THE CSS HUNLEY

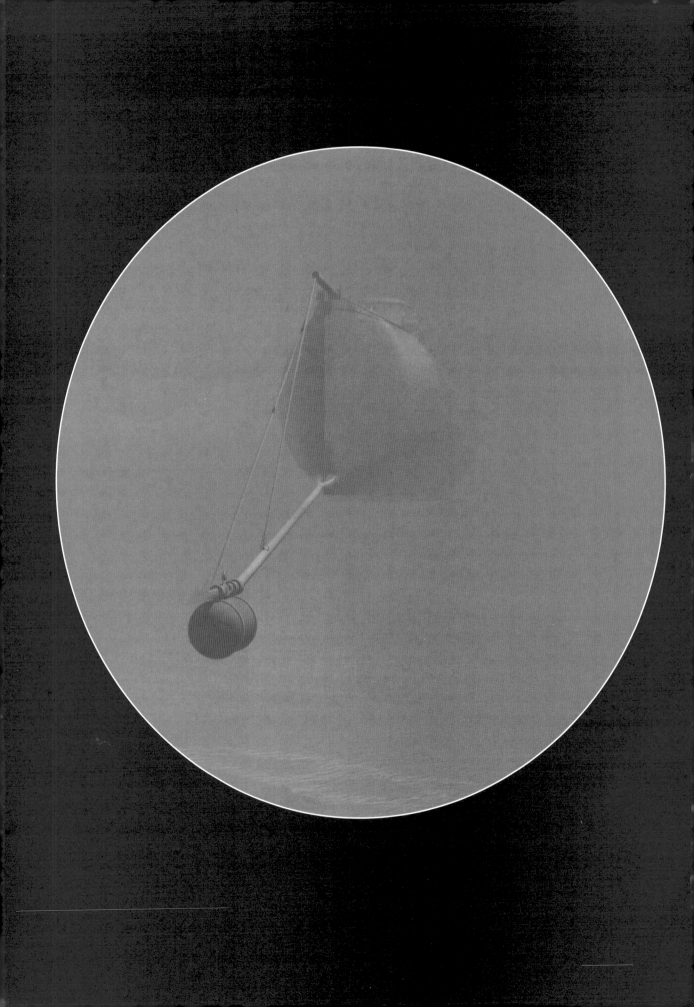

THE CSS HUNLEY

The Greatest Undersea Adventure of the Civil War

RICHARD BAK

UPDATED EDITION

Cooper Square Press

Computer-generated illustrations copyright © 1998 by Daniel Dowdey

"Beauregard: The Napoleon of the Confederacy" is adapted from an article by Gerard Patterson that originally appeared in *Civil War Times Illustrated*. Reprinted with the permission of Cowles Enthusiast Media, Inc. (History Group). A Primedia Publication copyright © *Civil War Times Illustrated* magazine.

The H. L. Hunley Archaeology Management Plan is reprinted with the permission of the South Carolina Institute of Archaeology and Anthropology Hunley Project Working Group.

Copyright © 1996 by SCIAA Hunley Project Working Group.

First Cooper Square Press edition 2003

This Cooper Square Press paperback edition of *The CSS Hunley* is an unabridged republication of the edition first published in Dallas, Texas in 1999, with the addition of a new postscript. It is reprinted by arrangement with the author.

Published by Cooper Square Press
A Member of the Rowman & Littlefield Publishing Group
200 Park Avenue South, Suite 1109
New York, New York 10003-1503
www.coopersquarepress.com

Distributed by National Book Network

A previous edition of this book was cataloged as follows by the Library of Congress

Bak, Richard, 1954–
    The CSS Hunley: the greatest undersea adventure of the Civil War / Richard Bak.
      p. cm.
   ISBN 0-8154-1260-6 (pbk.: alk. paper)
   1. H. L. Hunley (Submarine) 2. Submarines (Ships)—United States—History—19th century. 3. Confederate States of America. Navy—History. 4. Charleston (S.C.)—History—Civil War, 1861–1865. 5. United States—History—Civil War, 1861–1865—Naval operations—Submarine. I. Title.

E599.H4B35   1999
973.7'57—dc21
                                           99–18435

∞™ The paper used in this publication meets the minimum requirements of American National Standard for Information Sciences—Permanence of Paper for Printed Library Materials, ANSI/NISO Z39.48–1992.
Manufactured in the United States of America.

They were the first, so far as history records, in all the world to demonstrate the possibility of successfully operating a submarine torpedo boat, years before much attention had been given to the subject. The *Hunley* accomplished the purpose for which a submarine torpedo boat was designed, vis., to operate under water at sea, exploding a torpedo under and sinking the war vessel of an enemy in time of war....Submarine navigation arrived with the *Hunley*....

— William A. Alexander, 1903

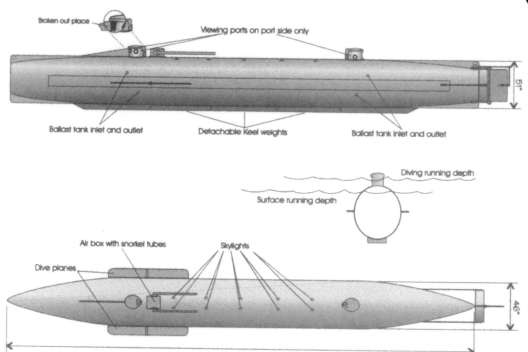

Broken out place

Viewing ports on port side only

Ballast tank inlet and outlet

Detachable Keel weights

Ballast tank inlet and outlet

5'

Diving running depth

Surface running depth

Air box with snorkel tubes

Skylights

Dive planes

46"

39'-6"

Based on recent measurements and findings by underwater archaeologists working with the S.C. Institute of Archaeology and Anthropology and the National Park Service.

ART WORK BY DAN DOWDEY
SC Hunley Commission and SCIAA

H. L. Hunley: owner & designer

Construction engineers:
James R. McClintock
William Alexander
Lt. George E. Dixon

Built: Spring 1863 at Park & Lyons machine shop, Mobile, Ala.

Transported to Charleston S.C., August 1863

Hull length: 39'- 6" Hull beam: 42" - Hull height: 48"

Propulsion unit: Hand- turned screw propeller

Speed: 4-5 knots

Crew: 9

Armament: 90 lb. torpedo

1st Commander: Lt. John Payne

2nd Commander: Lt. George Dixon

Destroyed the U.S.S Housatonic Feb. 17, 1864

Sank with all hands as they were returning to base Feb. 17, 1864

CONTENTS

April 12, 1861:
Confederate batteries bom-
bard Fort Sumter in
Charleston Harbor.

Chapter One

PIONEERS, PIRATES, AND PATRIOTS

*I*n the early summer of 1861, just a few weeks after war had started, a letter circulated in several Southern newspapers. It was written by Frances G. Smith, an Alabama inventor who claimed that the Confederacy was ideally suited for a new form of warfare:

> From the Chesapeake to the mouth of the Rio Grande, our coast is better fitted for submarine warfare than any other in the world. I would have every hostile keel chased from our coast by submarine propellers. The new vessel must be cigar shaped for speed—made of plate iron, joined without external rivet head; about thirty feet long, with a central section about 4 x 3 feet driven by a spiral propeller. The new Aneroid Barometer made for increased pressure will enable the adventurer easily to decide his exact distance below the surface.

Smith went on to state that he was "preparing a detailed memoir on submarine warfare, discussing matters not proper to be spoken of here, illustrated with drawings." Whatever happened to Smith's report, which he claimed to be making available to the mayors of all Southern maritime cities, is unknown. But as the rather broad description in his published letter made clear, the concept of traveling under the waves was neither far-fetched nor particularly original. Men had been tinkering with the idea throughout much of recorded history.

Such disparate figures as Alexander the Great and Leonardo da Vinci have been credited with various advances in the development of underwater mischief. Alexander allegedly descended to the bottom of the sea in 332 B.C. in a glass globe lined with donkey skins, taking along a couple of friends and some food for good measure. Less fantastic was the reported claim of da Vinci. The accomplished 15th-century inventor supposedly chose to keep details of his "military diving system" secret for fear that it would fall into the hands of "men who practice assassination at the bottom of the sea."

It was left to a rather obscure 16th-century Englishman named William Bourne to contribute the most influential primer on submarine physics. Bourne, a former naval gunner of humble birth and spotty education, made his living as an innkeeper. But he also wrote scientific articles for the general public. Bourne explained that a boat could submerge simply by becoming heavier than the amount of water it displaced, what is known as "negative buoyancy." A boat at negative buoyancy continues to sink (with the attendant loss of volume adding to the rate of sinking) until positive buoyancy is added. Inventing a boat that would sink and rise on demand, then, meant creating a method to change either the weight or the volume of the vessel. The solution of early submarine designers was to add and remove water from ballast chambers: allow the chambers to flood in order to sink, then expel the water—typically through a hand- or foot-operated "forcing" pump—to permit the boat to resurface.

In 1623 a Dutch chemist and mechanical engineer, Cornelius Van Drebbel, built what is generally considered the first working submarine. The vessel reportedly dove to a depth of fifteen feet in the Thames River, exciting his patron, King James I, who was present for the demonstration. Oars fitted in watertight sleeves provided propulsion, while navigation was aided by an on-board compass. Unlike da Vinci, Van Drebbel had no compunctions about practicing "assassination under the seas." His idea was to secretly attack an enemy ship at anchor by ramming it with an explosive attached to the end of a long pole, an anti-ship device that was still in vogue two hundred years later when another submarine pioneer, Horace Lawson Hunley, was born on the other side of the Atlantic.

U. S. Secretary of the Navy Gideon Welles (*right*) and his Confederate counterpart, Stephen Mallory.

New Orleans, the most populous city in the Confederacy, was also its most important port. Before the Civil War only New York had handled more goods; once the shooting started, the Yankees moved quickly to seize control of the gateway to the Mississippi River. In the fall of 1861 Captain David Farragut was brought out of retirement to assemble a fleet of warships in the Gulf of Mexico. It grew into the greatest in the history of the U. S. Navy to that date: 46 vessels sporting 348 guns and 21 mortars. By early 1862, a Federal army of 18,000 men also was moving into position for the inevitable land and sea assault on the Crescent City.

During this period, the deputy collector at the U. S. Customs House at Decatur and Canal streets was Horace L. Hunley, the namesake of what would become the first submarine in history to sink an enemy vessel. Hunley was perhaps not so much an early advocate of submarines as he was a zealot to the Confederacy's cause. To Hunley, such a vessel represented an adventurous, dangerous, but expedient means to an end, that end being the survival of the fledgling Confederacy and preservation of the "moonlight and magnolia" aristocratic Southern life he enjoyed and embodied.

Hunley was born on December 29, 1823, in Sumner County, Tennessee, but spent most of his life in New Orleans. He was well-educated, graduating from Tulane University in 1849, and wealthy, having made his fortune growing and selling sugar cane. He also was a lawyer and a legislator.

He demonstrated considerable fearlessness. In June of 1861 he headed a small expedition to Cuba, with an eye to securing a trade route over which weapons and munitions could be safely transferred between the Spanish-controlled island and Louisiana. Hunley's mission was judged a success by Confederate officials, though the subsequent fall of New Orleans would soon strangle this particular pipeline.

During the summer of 1861 the thirty-seven-year-old Hunley joined his brother-in-law, Robert R. Barrow, and two other New Orleans gentlemen—H. J. Leovy and James K. Scott, a fellow employee of the Customs House—in bankrolling a secret enterprise headed by James R. McClintock and Baxter Watson. The two maritime engineers operated a small shop at 31 Front Levee. The firm's principal business was manufacturing steam gauges and other engine parts, though upon the outbreak of the war they had secured a contract to design and build a pair of machines to produce minié balls, the hollow-based, lead conical bullets that became the standard infantry projectile of the war. For this they were paid $1,000. Unbeknownst to all but a handful of confidantes, at the same time the partners also were experimenting with plans for that most unorthodox of weapons, the submarine.

Little is known of either Watson or McClintock except that McClintock was reputed to be at one time before the war the youngest licensed riverboat captain on the Mississippi River. The genesis of their interest in submersibles is unknown, though it seems reasonable to assume that, because of their technical background and demonstrated curiosity and inventiveness, it dated from sometime before the outbreak of hostilities.

America, a nation of inventors, had from its earliest days demonstrated a natural curiosity about submersibles. David Bushnell had launched the first successful military submarine and mines during the Revolution, and such storied Yankee tinkerers as Robert Fulton and Samuel Colt had made contributions to the embryonic science of underwater warfare in the decades leading up to the Civil War. As with the ironclads, both the Union and the Confederacy—fearful of surrendering a huge advantage to the

The Confederate flag flies over vanquished Fort Sumter. Over the next four years, the fort would be reduced to rubble by shelling before finally being reclaimed by the Federals.

This group of cocky Confederates posed for the photographer inside Fort Sumter shortly after it fell in the spring of 1861.

other side—scrambled to be first with a workable combat submarine. The various private and governmental programs were cloaked in secrecy, but it wasn't long before occasional items made their way into the press.

In May 1861, Philadelphia papers reported on Brutus de Villeroi's strange vessel, first sighted in the Delaware River. "Never since the first flash of the bombardment of Fort Sumter," observed the *Philadelphia Evening Bulletin*, "has there been an excitement in the city equal to that which was caused by the capture of a mysterious vessel which was said to be an infernal machine, which was to be used for all sorts of treasonable purposes, including the trifling pastime of scuttling and blowing up government men-of-war." There was relief in the North when it was discovered that de Villeroi intended to present his services to President Lincoln on behalf of the Union.

But that October, the *New York Herald* reported on the first known submarine attack of the Civil War. The *Herald* described a Confederate vessel, made of iron and operated by two rebels hand-cranking a screw propeller, which one evening was brought from Norfolk, Virginia, to attack the *USS Minnesota*. The *Minnesota* was part of the North Atlantic Blockading Squadron and the flagship of Flag Officer Louis M. Goldsborough.

It has been only recently that the genesis of this vessel has been put together. According to historian Mark Ragan, a leading expert on Civil War submarines, in the summer of 1861 the Confederate Navy contracted with the Tredegar Iron Works in Richmond to build a pair of submersibles. One of them was the boat that, after several successful trial runs in the James River, attacked the *Minnesota*, wrote Ragan:

> The submarine, the brainchild of underwater explosives designer William Cheeney, was designed to be operated by two of its crew. The third man was provided with diving gear (known as "submarine armor") and stationed at the bow of the vessel in a special lockout chamber. A floating camoflaged hose attached to an air pump within the vessel provided oxygen to both the occupants and the diver outside. When the target ship came within reach of the diver, he would exit the craft and attach an explosive device to the bottom of the enemy ship, returning thereafter to the submarine. The boat would then withdraw a safe distance and detonate the device, either by a lanyard or timing mechanism. The ingenious and advanced aspects of this early war submarine were further substantiated when a diagram of the boat was captured by the Federals later in the war.

The mission failed, the result of that old standby, human error. The rebel craft intended to secure itself alongside the *Minnesota* by catching the ship's cable with a grapple. Instead, reported the *Herald*, it was "caught in the grappling always hanging from the jib-boom of the ship. This was taken by those inside [the submarine] for the chain cable, and when they thought they were under the bottom of the ship they made preparations for screwing the torpedo on the bilge, but, to their surprise, they found they were sadly mistaken, and they came near losing their lives as well as the machine."

The vessel escaped. The fleet was alarmed, as were more than a few Northerners. A depiction of the rebels' "infernal machine" appeared in the November 2, 1861, issue of *Harper's Weekly*, but within a week of its publication any hysteria over this particular

General Winfield Scott, commander in chief of the Union army in 1861, meets with Lincoln's cabinet. The 75-year-old Scott was the author of the "anaconda plan" that sought to split the Confederacy in two while strangling it economically with a blockade. Initially ridiculed, it ultimately was successfully adopted by the Union.

As a result of the little-known *"Trent* Affair," the Union found itself
on the verge of fighting a two-front war: one against the Confederacy
and the other against Great Britain. The controversy started on
November 7, 1861, when the Union warship *San Jacinto,* commanded
by Captain Charles Wilkes, intercepted the unarmed British mail
steamer *Trent* off Cuba. Aboard were two Southerners, John Slidell
and James M. Mason, who were en route to Paris and London,
respectively, to plead the Confederacy's cause. Slidell and Mason were
transferred to the *San Jacinto* and subsequently imprisoned. The
British, outraged by what they considered a violation of her freedom
of the seas, dispatched 8,000 troops to Canada. President Lincoln and
his secretary of state, William Seward, avoided bringing Great Britain
into the war by agreeing to release the two men from jail the following June. Slidell and Mason continued their interrupted mission but
were unable to convince either France or England to enter the conflict.

submarine was unwarranted.
Goldborough's orders to
squadron commanders to drag
the water for the tell-tale breath-
ing tubes evidently snared the
adventuresome craft, for three
weeks later a Union vessel at the
mouth of the James River
reported air tubes in its drag
rope. Whoever had depended
on those tubes would have
quickly drowned.

As another way of correcting
the imbalance between its nas-
cent, undersized navy and the
Union fleet, the Confederacy
took the highly controversial
step of authorizing privateers. In
his proclamation of April 17,
1861, Jefferson Davis stirred up
a hornet's nest by offering letters
of marque and reprisal. These
certificates of authorization,
banned internationally by the
1856 Declaration of Paris
(although the United States was
not a signatory), allowed citizens to arm privately owned vessels and attack enemy shipping.

Suddenly the waterfronts of
every Southern port city were
alive with whispered plans and loud boasts. Few activities could be
more dashing and adventurous—to say nothing of profitable—than
capturing an enemy merchant ship and its cargo. New Orleans,
with its long, colorful history of banditry stretching back to the
days of Jean Lafitte, embraced Davis's encouragement to plunder
Union commerce. Within five days of his proclamation the *Daily
Crescent* informed citizens that "there are two large and fast sailing
schooners fitting out at this city for the privateering business." The

A Northern artist visualized what a Confederate submarine looked like in the November 2, 1861, issue of *Harper's Weekly*.

newspaper reported that blank applications for letters of marque were available at Walter H. Peters's office at 50 Camp Street. Within weeks the office of the Confederate Secretary of the Navy was flooded with a reported three thousand applications. Only Charleston rivaled New Orleans in the number sent.

The likes of Lafitte were on Lincoln's mind when he denounced privateers as pirates, not patriots. The president warned that when captured, the crews of such ships would be treated according to longstanding maritime law: they would be hanged. Davis responded with the threat of reprisals.

Davis's proclamation was officially approved by the Confederate Congress on May 6, 1861. Twelve days later, in a room above the New Merchant Exchange Building in New Orleans, Watson and McClintock attended a noontime meeting of local men interested in fitting out their vessels as privateers. The young engineers listened attentively but said nothing of submarines at this gathering. Their silence was understandable; spies and busybodies were everywhere. About this time E. P. Doer, a New York native living in New Orleans,

Horace Lawson Hunley.

The U. S. Customs House in New Orleans, shown under construction in 1860. The supervising engineer was Captain P. G. T. Beauregard.

warned Washington that a submarine boat was being built in the city and would be used to attack Union vessels at the mouth of the Mississippi.

The Watson-McClintock shop was not far from the Leeds Foundry, an establishment owned and operated by the Confederate government. The foundry, located at the corner of Fourcher and Delord streets, was busily casting artillery pieces for the army. It also was involved in several privateering projects, including installing steam engines into the ironclad *Louisiana*. Despite being swamped by a backlog of orders, time and resources were devoted to creating a reality out of Watson and McClintock's vision.

Throughout the fall of 1861 and into early 1862, foundry employees worked diligently on the vessel. Large sheets of quarter-inch-thick plate, typically used in the construction of steam boilers, were bolted to an iron frame, producing an elongated craft with a rounded keel, deck, and sides. Its shape was most typically described as being like that of "an oversized cigar." Workers, looking to create as smooth a surface as possible, counter-sunk the hundreds of exterior bolt heads into the hull—a time-consuming task that designers hoped would pay off in increased speed.

There was no superstructure as in traditional surface vessels, merely a torso-squeezing hatchway, just eighteen inches around, installed amidship. There was no pilot house to assist navigation, either; a pair of glass-covered portholes offered the only opportunity for directional observations.

LINCOLN'S SUBMARINES

Abraham Lincoln may have grown up on the frontier, but the experiences and interests of the log-splitter in the White House were not limited entirely to the land. When he was nineteen, he and a local merchant had piloted a flatboat loaded with goods down the Ohio and Mississippi Rivers from Indiana to New Orleans, a three-month trip. A man of practical intelligence and wide-ranging curiosity, Lincoln later was granted a U. S. patent for an invention that lifted boats over shoals by means of "buoyant air chambers." So when a French engineer named Brutus de Villeroi offered his submarine to the Union cause, the president was enthusiastic.

"I propose to you a new arm of war," de Villeroi wrote Lincoln in September 1861, "as formidable as it is economical. Submarine navigation which has been sometimes attempted, but as all know without results, owing to want of suitable opportunities, is now a problematical thing no more."

De Villeroi had first experimented with submersibles in his native Nantes, France's premier port. There, in 1832, he had built his first three-man submarine; three years later he reportedly submerged in a ten-foot craft for two hours. (Interestingly, a boy named Jules Verne lived in Nantes at the time. It's not known whether the youngster observed any of Villeroi's experimental dives. But Verne displayed a life-long fascination with the sea and in 1869 published his best known book, *Twenty Thousand Leagues Under the Sea*, the classic tale of the eccentric Captain Nemo and his electric-powered submarine, the *Nautilus*.)

After unsuccessfully trying to sell a submarine to France during the Crimean War, de Villeroi moved to Philadelphia in 1859, hoping to find a more receptive audience for his invention. There he built a thirty-three-foot craft which he reportedly took to a depth of twenty feet for three hours. In May 1861, de Villeroi demonstrated his boat at the Philadelphia Navy Yard. Among those impressed was a reporter allowed a peek inside the strange underwater warship:

Lincoln was an early submarine enthusiast.

Fig. 3.

A sketch of the *Alligator*, the U. S. Navy's first submarine boat.

We suddenly found ourselves squatting inside a cigar shaped iron vessel, about four feet in diameter. There was a crank for the purpose of operating upon the propeller . . ., apparatus for steering rods, connected with fins outside, which could be moved at pleasure, and which had something to do with steadying and sinking the craft. There were pumps, brass faucets, pigs of ballast lead, and numerous other things, which might be intended for infernal or humane purposes for aught we know.

In November 1861, the Navy Department negotiated a $14,000 contract for Philadelphia contractor Martin Thomas to build a larger version of de Villeroi's submarine. Called the *Alligator*, it had an air-purification system and chambers from which divers could leave the submerged ship and attach explosive charges to the hulls of enemy ships. For all its modern features, the *Alligator*'s method of propulsion was no more sophisticated than in the days of the galley ships. To achieve a top speed of less than four knots an hour, sixteen oarsmen grunted and groaned over eight sets of self-feathering oars, whose hinged blades opened on the power stroke and closed on the return.

The *Alligator*, forty-five feet long and sixty-six inches from keel to deck, was completed the following April. This was too late to take on the Confederate ironclad *Virginia* but in time to be towed to Hampton Roads, Virginia, and deployed against the strategic James River Bridge.

In this mission the *Alligator* failed miserably. Needing a minimum draft of seven and a half feet to operate fully submerged, the submarine found itself dangerously exposed as it slowly navigated shallow stretches of the James River. Disgusted Navy officials had the vessel towed to the Washington Navy Yard, where its oars were replaced with a hand-cranked screw propeller. A demonstration of the retrofitted vessel in the Potomac River was attended by Lincoln, who continued to be convinced of its potential. However, on April 2, 1863, while it was being towed to join the blockading fleet off Charleston, it went down in a storm.

It was back to the drawing board. Not that the Federal government suffered from a lack of ideas. The flood of diagrams submitted during the war by civilian and military inventors—some crackpot, others scientifically sound—caused a committee to be formed in early 1863 to handle them. Committee members, appointed by Secretary of the Navy Gideon Welles, were charged with handling "all plans and inventions submitted to the Navy Department" and, whenever warranted, "to call in other experts" to judge their feasibility.

One idea that Lincoln took an intense interest in was Washington inventor Pascal Plant's rocket-driven submarine. After it was judged unfeasible, Plant responded with plans for a rocket-driven torpedo, something never seen before in warfare.

And perhaps for good reason. A test arranged in late 1862 resulted in Plant's rockets blowing up a mudbank and a schooner, neither of which was an intended target. In January 1863, Plant was given one last chance before the Navy brass. This time his rocket, instead of zipping underwater to its target, skipped like a rock across the water and screamed into the sky, before splashing down a hundred yards downriver.

The submarine committee was chaired by Rear Admiral Charles H. Davis, a Harvard-educated officer who Secretary Welles privately considered to be "more of a schol-ar than a sailor." Not long after Plant's rocket-torpedo debacle, Davis recommended funding for a submersible designed by a resourceful Massachusetts professor named Horstford. His was an ambitious design, calling for a fifty-five-foot vessel capable of holding twenty-six men. The professor's plans included a feature missing from other submarines of the period—a periscope. As Horstford explained, "A telescope with reflectors will be passed through a stuffing box in the top to any required height, by which the relative positions of objects may be ascertained without exposure of the vessel."

Hortsford's invention was most notable for its clever approach to the lingering problem of air purification. As one observer described it, a "tank of oxygen gas, compressed to one-fifteenth its volume was used. [Hortsford] employed a great surface of woolen cloth, which passed over pulleys and was dipped in lime water. A blower kept the air moving over the wet surface. The lime water absorbed the carbonic acid gas. As this gas is absorbed and a small amount of

Samuel Eakins commanded the *Alligator* in 1862–63.

oxygen liberated, the air may be kept nearly at normal purity."

Despite high hopes for Hortsford's unnamed vessel, however, the finished product proved impractical when it was tested in 1864.

Curiously, the U. S. Navy may well have employed a couple of working submarines in the fall of 1863, shortly after the *H. L. Hunley* was moved from Mobile, Alabama, to Charleston, South Carolina, with a view to breaking the Union blockade of the harbor. In August 1863, Admiral John Dahlgren, commander of the South Atlantic Blockading Squadron, wrote Secretary Welles for "a vessel constructed of corrugated iron, fashioned like a boat, but closed perfectly on top, so that it could be submerged very quickly." It would be used to help remove harbor obstructions.

So far, proof of their existence is fragmentary. No official Union documents regarding them have come to light—not suprising, given the highly confidential nature of submarine development on both sides. However, three separate mentions in Confederate dispatches in October 1863 describe two "nondescript affairs . . . elliptical in shape, low in the water and flush deck" operating with the Federal fleet off Charleston.

Nothing else is known of these Union craft—their origin, their size, their crews, their mission, their fate. They remain, like so many underwater adventures of the Civil War, submerged in secrecy and mystery.

Power was provided by a hand-turned spiral propeller attached to the stern, while two iron "flippers"—thirty-inch-long diving planes—were placed on either side of the hull near the bow. The planes were connected to a shaft to be controlled from within the confines of the narrow hull. Theoretically, the planes—along with the opening and pumping out of the ballast tanks—would allow the vessel to quickly submerge and resurface whenever the crew wanted.

The submarine, whose hull was painted black to camoflage it as it ran beneath the waves, held four men. The spartan interior was little better than a cave. Crew members sat upon U-shaped brackets bolted into the floor, turning a large crank in the semi-darkness. The only light was provided by candles. When the vessel was partially submerged, fresh air could be introduced into the stuffy chambers through a length of rubber tube called the "breather." The top end of this primitive snorkel broke the surface by use of an attached wooden float; a stop-cock inside the hose prevented water from rushing in once the craft was fully submerged.

In February 1862, under great secrecy, horses hauled the craft, now known as the *Pioneer*, to the Government Navy Yard at New Basin for its first tests. Only those men intimately involved with the vessel's financing and production were allowed to join the handful of military officials for the early trials.

The underwater runs were piloted by James K. Scott. Outside of a few small leaks (which were quickly fixed with generous applications of beeswax and tar), the vessel proved watertight and very capable.

"This boat demonstrated to us the fact that we could construct a boat that would move in any direction desired, and at any distance from the surface," McClintock recalled in a postwar letter to underwater explosives expert Matthew Fontaine Maury.

However, McClintock noted, there were problems with steering. The magnetic needle on the navigational compass—the sole instrument on board—fluttered erratically inside the iron hull of the *Pioneer*, making accurate readings impossible.

"As we were unable to see objects after passing under the water," McClintock continued in his letter to Maury, "the boat was steered by a compass, which at times acted so slow, that the boat would at times alter her course for one or two minutes before it

General Mansfield Lovell was the military commander of New Orleans. Lovell liked to drink and brag about the city's defenses, but after New Orleans easily fell to the Federal fleet in the spring of 1862, he was roundly scorned and relieved of command. A subsequent board of inquiry resulted in no finding of incompetence, but his military career was ruined.

Robert Fulton's 1798 submersible, the *Nautilus*. Its name would prove far more enduring than the vessel itself, being adopted by Jules Verne's fictional Captain Nemo and the U. S. Navy for its first atomic-powered submarine.

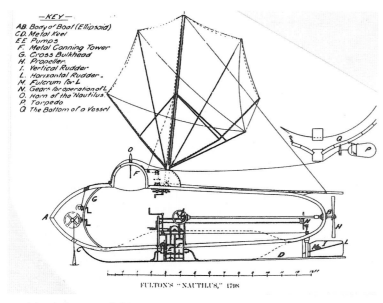

—KEY—
AB. Body of Boat (Ellipsoid)
CD. Metal Keel
EE. Pumps
F. Metal Conning Tower
G. Cross Bulkhead
H. Propeller
I. Vertical Rudder
L. Horizontal Rudder
M. Fulcrum for L
N. Gears for operation of L
O. Horn of the Nautilus
P. Torpedo
Q. The Bottom of a Vessel

FULTON'S "NAUTILUS," 1798

Nothing is known of this 1814 submarine, found in the notebook of Samuel Colt, except that it never graduated beyond the wishful thinking stage.

would be discovered, thus losing the direct course and so compel the operator to come to the top of the water more frequently than he otherwise would."

The malfunctioning compass frustrated Scott, who tested several other navigational devices. None worked to the skipper's satisfaction. Ultimately he resigned himself to coming to the surface every few minutes for a visual sighting and a correction in course. This was hardly an ideal solution, of course, because the element of surprise could be compromised once the *Pioneer* embarked on real missions against enemy ships. But crew members, who labored like galley slaves at the hand crank, appreciated these periodic resurfacings, for they got a brief respite from their backbreaking work and could gulp the fresh air brought into the oxygen-depleted hull. The problems of a limited air supply and a quickly exhausted crew would plague the *Pioneer* and all submarines built during the war.

More extensive testing took place in the deeper waters of Lake Pontchartrain, north of New Orleans. One day in March, the *Pioneer* underwent the most crucial part of its experimentation: safely delivering and triggering an explosive device against a surface craft. For this the *Pioner* had a circular notch in its bow, into which a long pine spar, a torpedo at its tip, could be snugly fitted.

The target in this test attack was a wooden barge moored in the middle of the lake. Scott, at the helm of the *Pioneer*, took a careful reading of the position before ordering the ballast tanks opened. With this the *Pioneer* slipped under the water and quietly glided toward its target.

There was a long period of silence, during which observers openly fretted that something had happened to the strange underwater craft. Suddenly an explosion rended the placid sky and water. The barge was blown "so high," wrote J. Thomas Scharf in his postwar study of the Confederate navy, "that only a few splinters were heard from."

According to a postwar statement from McClintock, in subsequent demonstrations the *Pioneer* also successfully attacked a number of other targets, including a schooner. The backers of the *Pioneer*, immensely pleased with the vessel's performance, officially named Scott captain and applied for a letter of marque. The formal application read:

To the Hon. Secretary of the Confederate States of America.

Sir:

Application is hereby made for a commission of authority in the name of the Government of these States, to issue the undersigned as commander of the submarine boat called the *Pioneer* for authority to cruise the high seas, bays, rivers, estuaries, etc, in the name of the Government, and aid said Government by the destruction or capture of any and all vessels opposed to or at war with said Confederate States, and to aid in repelling its enemies.

Said vessel is commanded by John K. Scott, who is a citizen of New Orleans and of this Confederacy. Said vessel was built at New Orleans in the year 1862; is a propeller; is thirty-four feet in length; is four feet breadth; is 4 feet deep. She measures about four tons; has rounded conical ends and is painted black. She is owned by Robert R. Barrow, Baxter Wtason, and James R. McClintock, all of this city of New Orleans. She will carry a magazine of explosive matter, and will be manned by two men or more.

And I hereby promise to be vigilant and zealous in employing said vessel for the purpose aforesaid and abide by all laws and instructions and at all times acknowledge the authority of the Government of said States and its lawful agent and officers.

Considering his bond the undersigned prays for the issuance of a commission or letter of marque.

(signed) John K. Scott

The letter of marque was granted on March 31, 1862, with Hunley and H. J. Leovy posting the $5,000 bond. The commission read as follows:

Confederate States of America
State of Louisiana,
City of New Orleans.

Jefferson Davis hoped to even the odds between the two navies by issuing letters of marque, authorizing privately owned vessels to attack Northern merchant ships.

JEFFERSON DAVIS,
President of the Confederate States of America.

To all Who shall see these Presents---Greeting:

Know Ye, That by virtue of the power vested in me by law, I have commissioned, and do hereby commission, have authorized, and do hereby authorize the _____ vessel called the _____ (more particularly described in the schedule hereunto annexed,) whereof _____ is Commander, to act as a private armed vessel in the service of the CONFEDERATE STATES, on the high seas, against the United States of America, their Ships, Vessels, Goods and Effects, and those of their citizens, during the pendency of the War now existing between the said CONFEDERATE STATES and the said United States.

This Commission to continue in force until revoked by the President of the CONFEDERATE STATES for the time being.

Schedule of Description of the Vessel.

NAME, _____

TONNAGE, _____

ARMAMENT, _____

NO. OF CREW, _____

Given under my hand and the Seal of the CONFEDERATE STATES at Montgomery, this _____ day of _____ A. D. 1861.

BY THE PRESIDENT: _____

Secretary of State.

Be it remembered that on this 29th day of the month of March in the year 1862, before me, Walter Hicks Peters, notary public, in and for this city and parish duly commissioned and qualified:

Personally came and appeared the above-named John K. Scott, applicant for the issuance of a letter of marque or commission to him as commander or captain of the vessel called the *Pioneer*, which appearer being known to me, and being by me duly sworn, says that he has accurately described the said vessel, her armament, number of crew, and the object and purpose in which said vessel is to be engaged, and that he will support the laws and constitution of said Confederate States, and obey all lawful commands of said Government and its officers.

So help me God.
(signed) John K. Scott

Sworn to me and subscribed to before me this 29th March, A.D., 1862.

(signed) Walter Hicks Peters.

Obtaining a letter of marque was not as common as might be supposed. Historians have been able to find only fifty-two granted between 1861 and 1864; of these, evidence points to only twenty-eight vessels actually operating as privateers.

The *Pioneer* proved to be unique—the only submarine to be sanctioned a privateer during the Civil War. As such, the motives of its backers can't be questioned, for a privateer was entitled to a share of any proceeds from the sale of the captured enemy ship and its cargo, as determined by a prize court. There obviously was no room aboard the *Pioneer* to haul away spoils of war; moreover, its construction made it incapable of cruising the high seas in search of merchant ships. It appears that Hunley and his associates were motivated purely by patriotism, not profit.

The *Pioneer*'s letter of marque was granted shortly after the controversy surrounding the use of privateers had reached a climax of

According to this sketch that appeared in *Harper's Weekly*, Northern ships chasing privateers should be equipped with their own gallows—the easier to hang their piratical crews.

James R. McClintock, a gifted marine engineer, helped build and operate the South's first submarines—first in New Orleans, then in Mobile and Charleston.

:6 feet long.
Fish shaped.

3½ feet wide
5 feet deep

Hunley's Fish Fin Torpedo.
Boat.
made of galvanised iron worked
by a hand crank

This crude drawing depicts the submarine built by James McClintock and Baxter Watson in New Orleans in 1861–62. Financial backers included Horace Hunley, a local sugar broker whose name adorns this sketch. Actually, "Hunley's Fish Fin Torpedo Boat" was called the *Pioneer*.

sorts with the resolution of a *cause celebre* known as the *Enchantress* Affair.

In Charleston, a forty-three-year-old merchantman named Louis Coxetter had outfitted a former slave ship with five ancient British cannon, renamed it the *Jefferson Davis*, and set about wreaking havoc along the Atlantic seaboard. During the summer of 1861 the *Jefferson Davis* took nine Northern vessels as prizes, including the merchant schooner *Enchantress* off the coast of southern Delaware. A prize crew of five seamen under the command of Walter W. Smith took control of the ship and confiscated its $13,000 worth of cargo. Two weeks later, however, the *Enchantress* was captured by the *USS Albatross*. Smith and his crew were slapped in irons and put on trial for their lives in Philadelphia circuit court.

Matthew Fontaine Maury.

The captured rebels were found guilty of piracy by a civilian jury and sentenced to death. This provoked Judah P. Benjamin, the acting Confederate secretary of war, to order a lottery among captured Union officers to determine which of them would be executed in kind. The list grew to include the fifteen highest-ranking officers, each of whom represented a captured Southern seaman awaiting execution in Northern jails.

THE IRONCLADS

As the first truly modern conflict, the Civil War saw the unprecedented use of such innovative naval weaponry as submarines, semisubmersibles (commonly called "Davids") and floating mines ("torpedos"). But nothing was more revolutionary than the ironclad, whose success marked an end to the era of wooden ships and sails.

The most famous naval battle in American history occurred early in the war between the *USS Monitor* and the *CSS Virginia*. This showdown between opposing ironclads was judged a draw, but their encounter forever changed the face of naval warfare.

The *Virginia* actually was the converted Union frigate *Merrimac*, which had been burned to the waterline during the U. S. Navy's hasty abandonment of the Norfolk Navy Yard in Gosport, Virginia, in the first weeks of the war. Despite the damage, the *Merrimac* proved to be a prize catch for the Confederate Navy. Its secretary, former Florida senator Stephen R. Mallory, had observed with great interest the introduction of armored ships into the French and English navies during his prewar tenure as chairman of the Naval Affairs Committee. Mallory's original vision was to buy a half-dozen foreign-built ironclads, using them to smash the Union blockade of the 3,500 miles of Confederacy coastline. But when it quickly became apparent that neither of the feuding European powers was going to sell one of their armored vessels, Mallory had no choice but to order them built domestically, starting with the captured *Merrimac*.

Confederate designers used the hull and engines of the *Merrimac*, then constructed an armored superstructure that extended to just below the waterline. Inside the casemate were ten heavy guns; it also had a cast iron prow for ramming. Word began to leak to the North of this imposing vessel while it was still being built in dry dock. This caused great concern in Washington, where Mallory's inexperienced counterpart, Gideon Welles, capably guided by Assistant Secretary Gustavus Vasa Fox, was trying to rush through the Union's own ironclad building project.

In August 1861, a $275,000 contract was signed with John Ericcson to quickly design and build an armored warship to counter the Confederacy's coming ironclad threat. The Swedish-born inventor had fallen into disfavor with the government after one of his cannons had exploded during a demonstration in 1844, killing several observers, including the secretaries of state and navy. But events would soon make Ericcson a hero in the North.

Ericcson's steam-powered warship was launched as the *USS Monitor* on January 30, 1862. It

The fall of the Norfolk Navy Yard in Gosport, Virginia, was an unexpected but extremely valuable prize for the Confederacy. It was there that the captured Union frigate, the *Merrimac*, was remodeled into the ironclad *CSS Virginia*.

REMODELING THE
"MERRIMAC" AT THE GOSPORT
NAVY YARD.

President Lincoln created the position of assistant secretary of the U. S. Navy for Gustavus Vasa Fox, whose administrative experience and diplomatic manner made him an indispensible number-two man to Navy Secretary Gideon Welles. It was Fox who sold Welles on the idea of using ironclads in battle.

John Ericsson, designer of the *Monitor*.

was aptly described as a "cheesebox on a raft." It featured a unique revolving gun turret — made of eight-inch-thick iron plate and weighing a whopping 120 tons — topping a 172-foot-long wooden hull that rested almost entirely below the waterline. The *Monitor* was armed with two 11-inch Dahlgren smoothbores capable of firing a 180-pound iron ball. Critics called it an "iron coffin" and expected it to immediately sink, but Ericcson confidently stood on the *Monitor*'s deck as the chocks were pulled and the iron-

The crew of the *Monitor*.

clad settled easily into New York's East River.

A fortnight later, the *Merrimac* was launched and rechristened the *Virginia*. In command was Captain Franklin Buchanan, a crusty, scrappy forty-six-year veteran of the U. S. Navy and the first superintendent of the Naval Academy. "Old Buck" had resigned his commission to serve his native Maryland. Buchanan designated the vessel flagship of the James River Squadron and on March 8, 1862, immediately set out to fight his former employer.

Hampton Roads, Virginia, was a dozen miles downriver of the Norfolk Navy Yard. As Union bluejackets aboard the wooden men-of-war looked on in amazement, the lumbering *Virginia* headed straight for them. Point-blank broadsides had little effect on the Confederate ironclad, as over the next several hours it rammed and sank the *Cumberland*, wounded the *Minnesota*, and blew the *Congress* to pieces. The *Virginia* might have inflicted even more damage, but darkness and several casualties — including the irrepressible Buchanan, who was wounded while firing a rifle at the *Congress* — forced a withdrawal. But this armored scourge was certain to renew its attack the following morning.

When it did, it was met by the *Monitor*, which had arrived overnight after being towed on a perilous ocean voyage from the Brooklyn Navy Yard to Hampton Roads. For more than four hours the two evenly matched ironclads circled and raked each other, sometimes from just a few feet away. With both ships hampered by inexperienced gun crews, neither side was able to deliver a knockout blow. Only after the *Monitor*'s captain was blinded by flying splinters and the *Virginia* developed a leak in its bow did the ships finally break off the engagement.

Although indecisive, the battle was immediately recognized as a landmark. Washington, which had earlier been in a panic that the *Virginia* would steam unmolested up the Potomac, now was gripped with "*Monitor* fever." From now on all naval resources would be directed towards constructing a fleet of ironclads, which inevitably came to be known by the generic name of "monitors." Similarly, the Confederate government became more convinced than ever that ironclads were the answer to breaking the blockade, though the lack of resources would result in Southern shipyards producing only one-third as many as the North.

The ironclads proved not to be as invincible as originally thought. In a famous action on April 7, 1863, nine of them attacked Confederate forts around Charleston and were no match for

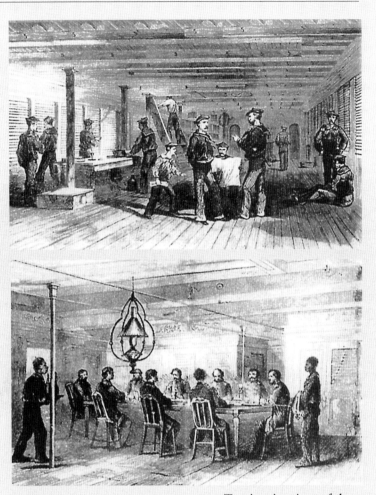

the Rebels' expertly placed artillery fire. Moreover, because of their low drafts, the ungainly ironclads had to be towed through ocean waters. They were susceptible to foundering — a fate that claimed the *Monitor* on New Year's Eve, 1862, as it was being towed to Charleston for blockade duty.

At that the *Monitor* outlived its famous opponent by seven months. With the fall of Norfolk in the spring of 1862, the *Virginia* was run aground and burned to avoid its falling into enemy hands.

Two interior views of the *USS Montauk*, one of some sixty ironclads built following the success of the *Monitor* at Hampton Roads. The top sketch shows the berth deck of the ironclad, while the bottom shows the ward room. Remarkably durable, several ironclads remained in service through the 1920s.

The Confederate Navy's naval mines were simple but effective devices called "torpedoes." The powder-filled metal canisters were floated by empty wooden kegs and set off by electrical fuses.

In the greatest loss of life caused by a torpedo during the war, ninety-three sailors died when the *USS Tecumseh* struck a Confederate mine at Mobile Bay in 1864.

Painted into a corner, President Lincoln finally decided that the captured crewmen would be transferred from civilian jails to military prisons and treated as prisoners of war. This fended off a tit-for-tat round of executions between the two belligerent nations. It was a small legal and diplomatic victory for the Confederacy, though it had little time remaining in which to fully enjoy its advantages. The subsequent fall of New Orleans, along with the strengthened Union blockade, led to a drastic fall-off in privateering activity. Although some vessels became blockade runners or were commissioned as men-of-war, others were captured or scuttled.

Among those scuttled was the *Pioneer*, which never had a chance to confront Farragut's armada. The Federal assault on New Orleans began on April 16, 1862, with a massive mortar bombardment of Forts Jackson and St. John, located 75 miles downstream of the city. After four days of softening up the shore defenses, Union gunboats skirted the battered forts and sliced up the Mississippi, paving the way for Farragut's larger warships. The badly outnumbered and outgunned Confederate fleet included the partially completed ironclad *Louisiana* and the single-gun ram *Manassas*, the South's first all-metal ship. Although they were unable to influence the outcome of this particular engagement, their presence fighting Farragut's all-wooden flotilla sent a message that the age of "wooden ships and iron men" was quickly passing.

By April 24 Federal warships were converging on a city filled with smoke, explosions, and panic. That day the *Pioneer*'s investors, unwilling to have their pride and joy fall into the hands

The cigar-shaped *Manassas*, the South's first all-metal ship, was employed as a ram during the battle for New Orleans.

In the Battle of Forts Jackson and St. Philip, Union warships fought their way past moored Confederate hulks, fire rafts, and ironclads. They continued 70 miles up the Mississippi, forcing the surrender of New Orleans on April 25, 1862.

of Union forces, hurriedly cut holes into it and sank it in the New Basin Canal. Hunley, Watson, and McClintock then hastily gathered together whatever mechanical drawings and personal belongings they could and fell in with the thousands of soldiers and civilians fleeing the Federal advance. The following day a pair of brave Union officers disembarked on the steamboat landing, strode through a jeering mob to city hall, and demanded the city's surrender.

⚓

In 1879, a crew dredging a channel stumbled across a corroding hull. Intrigued, but unaware of its potential historical significance, they simply moved it to the banks of the Mississippi River, where it lay forgotten for years. In 1909, a Confederate veterans group recovered the weed-choked hulk, announced that it was the long-lost *Pioneer*, and exhibited it at a local soldiers home. In the late 1950s the vessel was put on display at the Louisiana State Museum, where the odd-looking contraption has fascinated visitors to New Orleans's French Quarter ever since.

As it turns out, the egg-shaped vessel is undoubtedly a submarine produced in New Orleans at some point before the fall of the city. But it is not the *Pioneer*.

The real *Pioneer* was hauled out of the water by Federal troops

Rear Admiral David G. Farragut.

During the Battle of New Orleans, Admiral Farragut had his mortar schooners camoflage their masts with branches as they moved upriver toward two Confederate forts.

Raphael Semmes, captain of the *CSS Alabama*, was the ultimate commerce raider, capturing and sinking fifty-five prizes between 1862 and 1864. Hailed as a hero in the South and reviled as a pirate in the North, Semmes's rampage was halted when the *USS Kearsarge* sank the *Alabama* in a storied one-hour duel off the coast of Cherbourg, France, on June 19, 1864. Semmes was saved from drowning by a passing yacht and taken to England, from where he made his way back to the South. After the war he was arrested and charged with various crimes, including piracy and violating the rules of war, but he was eventually released. He returned to Mobile, where he practiced law until his death in 1877.

This egg-like vessel has long been thought to be James McClintock and Baxter Watson's first submarine, the *Pioneer*, though recent research indicates that it is almost certainly not. It is shown here being moved to the Lousiana State Museum in 1957.

not long after they occupied New Orleans. Several military engineers thoroughly examined the craft, including a fellow named G. W. Baird. "When a third assistant aboard the *Pensacola* during the Civil War," Baird wrote in 1902, "I had the pleasure of assisting Second Assistant Engineer Alfred Colin in the measurements and drawings of a submarine torpedo boat which had been fished out of the canal near the 'New Basin' between New Orleans and the Lake Pontchartrain."

Baird went on to describe the vessel:

> The boat was built of iron cut from old boilers, and was designed and built by Mr. McClintock, in his machine shop in the city of New Orleans. She was thirty feet in length; the middle body was cylindrical, ten feet long, and the ends were conical. She had a little conning tower with a manhole in the top, and small, circular, glass windows in its sides. She was propelled by a screw, which was operated by one man. She had vanes, the functions of which were those of the pectoral fins of a fish. The torpedo was of a clockwork type, and was intended to be screwed into the bottom of the enemy's ship. It was carried on top of the boat, and the screws employed were gimlet-pointed and tempered steel.
>
> Mr. McClintock (whom I met after the Civil War had ended) informed me that he had made several descents in his boat, in the lake, and succeeded in destroying a small schooner and several rafts. He stated that the U. S. Steamers *New London* and *Calhoun* had been a menace on the lake, and this gave rise to the torpedo boat; but before an attack was made the fleet of Farragut had captured New Orleans, and his boat was sunk to prevent her from falling into the hands of the enemy.

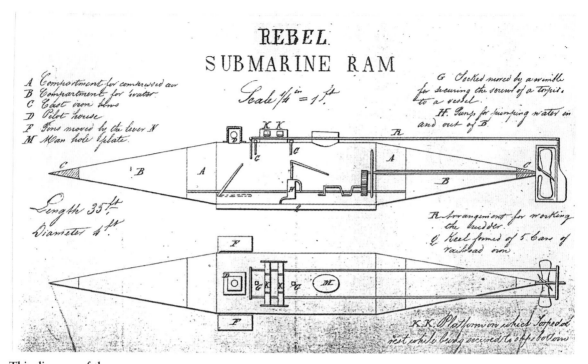

REBEL.
SUBMARINE RAM

This diagram of the *Pioneer* was drawn by William Shock, engineer on the *USS Pensacola*, shortly after New Orleans fell to Union forces in April 1862.

The description of the submarine that Baird and his colleagues examined does not match that of the one on display at the museum. One of the most obvious of several discrepancies is the length of the museum's vessel. Measuring nineteen feet, six inches from bow to stern, it is only two-thirds as long as the *Pioneer* was reliably reported to be. Some historians now believe the museum's submarine is probably the one E. P. Doer was referring to in his warning letter to Secretary of the Navy Gideon Welles. Its builder remains a mystery.

What happened to the *Pioneer*? The February 15, 1868, edition of the *New Orleans Picayune* carried the following advertisement:

AUCTION SALES

A torpedo boat, which was built in this city or hereabouts during the war, and which is now lying on the banks of the New Canal, near Claiborne street, is to be sold at public auction to-day, by the United States authorities, at 12 o'clock, at the Canal street entrance of the Custom House. The boat in question, which is built of iron and weighs about two tons, was sunk in the Canal about the time of the occupation of the city by the Federal forces, in 1862. It was built as an experiment, and was never fully perfected, and is only valuable now for the machinery and iron which is in and about it.

That day the *Pioneer*, which according to the newspaper had originally cost $2,600 to build, was sold for scrap for $43. The buyer is unknown, but it most certainly wasn't James K. Scott. The *Pioneer*'s captain had ended his business association with Hunley, McClintock, and Watson after the fall of New Orleans, evidently coming to the conclusion that he was more likely to inflict damage on the enemy with a musket than with a torpedo. While his inventive friends looked for a fresh start in another Southern port city, Scott marched off to fight with a Louisiana infantry regiment and was never seen nor heard from again.

Admiral
Franklin
Buchanan
was in charge of
the Confederates'
defense of Mobile.

throughout. There was an endless stream of balls and dinner parties, and the many oyster bars and French restaurants continued servicing their clientele with nary an interruption.

Judging by the fondness with which many of the leading citizens of Mobile later remembered Hunley, the wealthy and well-connected transplant evidently threw himself into the gay social life of the city.

"Mobile had suffered very little from the war, and still carried on a brisk commerce with the outer world in spite of the blockade," Fitzgerald Ross noted during a visit in the third year of the war. "It is pleasantly situated on a broad plain, and has a beautiful prospect of the bay, from which it receives refreshing breezes. Large vessels cannot come directly to the city, but pass up Spanish River six miles round a marshy island into Mobile River, and then drop down to Mobile."

One day the visiting Englishman "went down the bay to visit the outer defences in a magnificent river-steamer." In addition to the governor, Admiral Franklin Buchanan "and other gentlemen and ladies were of the party," wrote Ross.

"A very good band of music from one of the regiments of the garrison played, and dancing was soon got up in the splendid saloon. They dance the 'finale' of the quadrille here with all sorts of figures—one of them like the last figure in the Lancers, walking round and giving the right and left hand alternately. Admiral Buchanan, who was looking on, joined in this, and naturally by doing so created a great deal of confusion and merriment, at which he was in high glee. He is immensely popular, and the young ladies all call him a charming old gentleman, although he is at least ten years too young to be an admiral in England."

It's not clear whether the gallant Buchanan, who had been

made commander of naval forces at Mobile shortly after the *Virginia*'s historic clash with the *Monitor*, ever crossed paths with Hunley, either socially or professionally. But Buchanan certainly knew of the highly secret project Hunley and his fellow investors were backing, because surviving letterbooks show that throughout 1863 the admiral occasionally exchanged correspondence with McClintock, Watson, and the secretary of the Confederate Navy concerning certain aspects of the *Pioneer II*.

Although Buchanan was willing to entertain just about any desperate measure that might lift the Federal blockade, his view of the the experimental vessel's seaworthiness resisted change. "I considered the whole affair as impracticable from the commencement," he would say after the Louisiana inventors' second diving machine sank and was irretrievably lost. But a third, more successful submarine would force him to change his mind.

Upon their arrival in the spring of 1862, Hunley and his companions found a city filled with workshops and foundries busily producing weapons, munitions, and other war essentials. After inquiring of several machine shops, they made connections with the reputable firm of Thomas Park and Thomas B. Lyons, whose spacious brick shop at the corner of Water and State streets boasted a foundry, large cranes, and just about everything else needed to build artillery engines for the Confederate government. Park and Lyons agreed to manufacture the *Pioneer*'s successor. During its

The Park and Lyons machine shop in Mobile, where the *Pioneer II* and the *Hunley* were built.

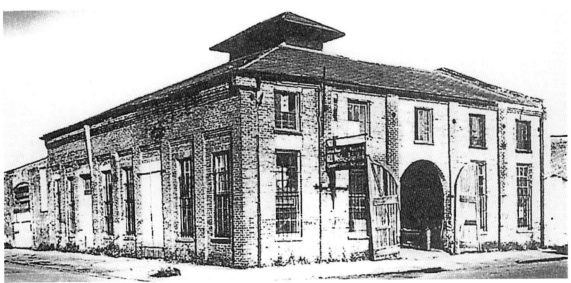

THE *TURTLE*:

The World's First Combat Submarine

During the American Revolution, eighty-eight years before the *Hunley* sank the *Housatonic*, an even more primitive submersible made history by staging the first submarine attacks on an enemy vessel. Although unsuccessful, David Bushnell's *Turtle* demonstrated the possibilities of a new kind of warfare launched from beneath the waves.

Bushnell grew up on a Connecticut farm, but it wasn't until his father died that the fledgling Yankee tinkerer was free to pursue his formal education. In 1775, at age thirty-three, he graduated from Yale University and immediately set to work perfecting his idea of an underwater gunpowder mine. His interest in building a submarine was secondary; he viewed such a vessel as merely the means of delivering the explosive to the target.

Bushnell's weaponry system was primitive but ingenious. It consisted of an oval-shaped box filled with 150 pounds of gunpowder, a detonating device, and a clock timer to trigger the explosive. The bomb (which was stored just behind the hatch) was to be attached to the hull of the enemy ship below the waterline. To keep it in place, the pilot would operate a long hand screw from within his cramped compartment to bore a hole into the timber. The submarine would then pull away, leaving the bit—to which the bomb was attached by a length of rope—behind in the wood. The timer was activated, giving the *Turtle* a maximum of twenty minutes to make its escape.

Bushnell's one-man submersible stood six feet high and seven feet long; it was shaped like a giant round clam. It was dubbed the *Turtle* because, according to one correspondent to the Continental Congress, "The Body, when standing upright in the position in which it is navigated, has the nearest resemblance to the two upper shells of a Tortoise joined together. . . ."

The *Turtle* descended and ascended through foot-operated inlet valves and outlet pumps. A 200-pound lead weight was stored under the keel for emergency ballast; it could be jettisoned should the *Turtle* need to make the surface in a pinch. A pair of brass tubes let fresh air in. Each tube was equipped with a float valve that kept water out when the boat dipped under the surface; there also was an internal check valve in the event the float valve failed. When submerged the craft's operator could depend on an oxygen supply of about thirty minutes.

Illumination inside the cramped compartment was problematical. In lieu of using a candle, which ate up the air supply, Bushnell equipped the eighteen-inch glass tube that served as a barometer with a phosphorescent cork of fox fire.

To propel the *Turtle*, Bushnell installed "a pair of oars fixed like the two opposite arms of a windmill, with which he can row forward, and turning them the opposite way, row the machine backward; another pair fixed upon the same model, with which he can row the machine round, either to the right or left, and a third, by which he can row the machine either up or down; all of which are turn'd by foot, like a spinning wheel." Through some vigorous hand-cranking, the operator could get the *Turtle* moving through the water as fast as three miles per hour.

The *Turtle* was operational by late 1775, but it wasn't until the following spring that it was ready to be employed against the enemy. One persistent problem was funding; another was training somebody to operate the vessel. Bushnell never did get wholly compensated for his time and expenses, and his first trainee—his brother, Ezra—lost his health after spending months mastering the difficult-to-operate craft. Luckily for Bushnell, he found a capable and courageous replacement in Sergeant Ezra Lee, a forty-five-year-old army volunteer from Lyme, Connecticut.

The British, thanks to a spy, knew the colonists were ready to

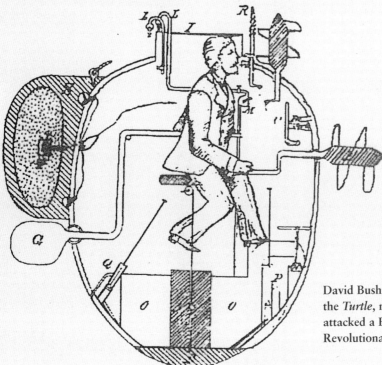

David Bushnell's one-man submarine, the *Turtle*, made history when it attacked a British vessel during the Revolutionary War.

launch some sort of novel machine against their fleet, but details were lacking.

On the evening of September 6, 1776, a couple of rowboats towed the *Turtle* into position. The target was the sixty-four-gun *Eagle*, the flagship of Admiral Sir Richard Howe and one of nearly 300 British vessels moored in New York harbor. The *Eagle* was anchored off Bedloe's Island (today known as Liberty Island, site of the Statue of Liberty). Sealed inside the *Turtle* was Sergeant Lee, who couldn't have wiggled out if he wanted to: strapping held the entry hatch water-tight and could only be removed with outside help.

Lee almost immediately lost his bearings in the darkness. To make matters worse, the strong outgoing tide soon had the *Turtle* sweeping past the fleet and headed out to open sea. Paddling for all he was worth, Lee worked the hand-cranks until his lungs and limbs felt as if they were going to explode. Finally, after two and a half hours of frantic effort, he was back in range of the fleet.

Lee picked out what he thought to be the *Eagle*, sub-merged, and went to work. Under the cover of night and several feet of water, he repeatedly tried to get the wooden drill to bite into the ship's hull. Now and then, he maneuvered his vessel to the sur-face to gulp in some fresh air before diving back to renew his efforts. By dawn he was exhaust-ed, disoriented, and probably suf-fering from carbon-dioxide poi-soning.

Legend has it that the unlucky submariner had to contend with the ship's copper-plated bottom, but British Naval records reveal that the *Eagle* was still six years away from receiving this protec-tion against the toredo worm. Lee may have simply attacked the wrong ship; if the ship was indeed the *Eagle*, Lee likely had struck an iron bolt or brace, not copper sheathing.

In any event, Lee was spotted as he made his return to friendly shores. A barge of British Marines pursued him. Figuring that he was

short life this second experimental submarine was alternately referred to as the *Pioneer II* and the *American Diver*.

Unlike the first go-around, which featured several investors, Hunley wholly financed the construction of this second model. The sum is unknown, but it must have been considerable, perhaps as much as $10,000 or $15,000. The interest of the cash-strapped Confederate government naturally was piqued by the project, but it could contribute only free labor and access to whatever facilities were needed to the cause.

about to be overcome by either his pursuers or fatigue, he armed the bomb and cast it off, looking to destroy himself and the submarine in the process. At this point luck finally fell Lee's way. The British, alarmed by the strange floating device, backed off, allowing him to escape. A short while later the bomb exploded, injuring nobody but creating a spectacular noise that could be heard as far away as Manhattan Island.

In the coming weeks Lee made at least one more attack, equally unsuccessful, before the *Turtle* fell into disuse because of lack of funding and Bushnell's own reservations about its practicality. Bushnell concentrated on floating mines and met with some success. In August 1777, one was hauled aboard the British frigate *Cerberus* by several curious sailors; it exploded, killing three men and destroying a nearby schooner. That December, Bushnell floated several of his keg-like mines down the Delaware River. One blew a boat to bits, causing British sol-diers to stand on the riverbank and excitedly shoot at anything that drifted past. The satirical poem, "Battle of the Kegs," was a result:

> Therefore prepare for bloody
>   war,
> The kegs must all be routed,
> Or surely we despised shall be
> And British valor doubted.

Nobody ever doubted the valor of Ezra Lee, who went on to fight in the battles of Trenton, Brandywine, and Monmouth before returning to Lyme, where he died in 1821. The *Turtle*'s attack on the *Eagle*, a staple of juvenile histories of the American Revolution for generations, under-scored the courage of all early sub-mariners. As George Washington, recalling Bushnell's "effort of genius" in a 1785 letter to Thomas Jefferson, wrote: "it is no easy matter to get a person hardy enough to encounter the variety of dangers to which [a submariner] must be exposed."

It was Hunley's good fortune to have come upon Park and Lyons just as a bright, young engineer, Lieutenant William A. Alexander, was assigned to temporary duty at the shop. Alexander had emigrated from England two years earlier, enlisting in Company A of the 21st Alabama Infantry Regiment. The outfit had taken a beating at the Battle of Shiloh, fought in middle Tennessee the first week of April 1862.

Alexander worked closely with McClintock and Watson, por-ing over drawings and brainstorming into the late hours of the

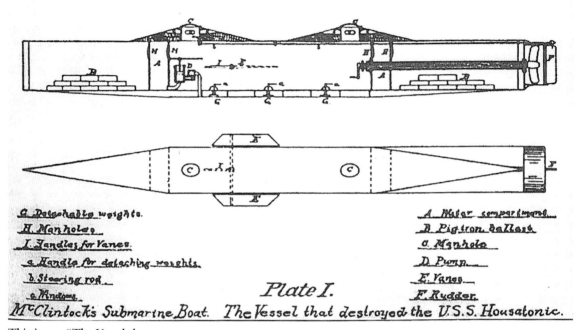

G. *Detachable weights.*
H. *Manholes.*
I. *Handles for Vanes.*
a. *Handle for detaching weights.*
b. *Steering rod.*
c. *Window.*

A. *Motor compartment.*
B. *Pig-iron Ballast.*
C. *Manhole.*
D. *Pump.*
E. *Vanes.*
F. *Rudder.*

Plate I.

McClintock's Submarine Boat. The Vessel that destroyed the U.S.S. Housatonic.

This is not "The Vessel that destroyed the U.S.S. Housatonic," as the legend beneath this diagram incorrectly states. Rather, it was the *Pioneer II*, also known as the *American Diver*, the second of three submarines with which Horace Hunley and James McClintock were involved.

night. Some of their sessions, to be sure, were pure blue-sky, but the men's enthusiasm could not be faulted. Their work continued through the summer and fall of 1862, with "much time and money lost," said McClintock, experimenting with the idea of using an electro-magnetic engine as the vessel's source of propulsion. Employing electricity for power was a revolutionary concept for the times, but the group's efforts were affected by the lack of material resources afflicting every aspect of Confederate war production.

They also worked on building a small but powerful steam engine. Theoretically, the fire inside the boiler would be extinguished before diving, the vessel running on the pent-up pressure. That idea also fell by the wayside. For all of their determination and creativity, the frustrated inventors ultimately had to return to that most basic mode of propulsion: a cramped crew of crankers.

The *Pioneer II* was built bigger than its predecessor to make room for the anticipated engine; instead it accomodated a larger crew. "I afterwards fitted cranks to turn the propeller by hand," he said, "working four men at a time, but the air being so closed, and the work so hard, that we were unable to get a speed sufficient to make the boat of service against vessels blockading this port."

McClintock stated that the finished model measured "thirty-six feet long, three feet wide and four feet high, twelve feet at each end was built tapering . . . to make her easy to pass through the water."

(According to a postwar recollection of Alexander, who was working from his memory, not drawings, the boat was five feet wide and
six feet deep.)

As with the original *Pioneer*, a pair of diving fins located on
either side of the bow controlled its ability to dive and return to the
surface. The new version had two hatchways instead of one, making it easier for the five crew members (or perhaps six; accounts
aren't clear) to enter and leave the claustrophobic belly of the boat.
The captain—evidently McClintock, though others probably commanded at times—had the benefit of a crude mercury gauge to
determine the vessel's depth. The only other piece of instrumenta-
tion was a compass.

As technologically advanced as the *Pioneer II* appeared, it
proved to be a major disappointment, particularly to Buchanan,
who listened doubtfully to claims that the new invention could be
the major force in lifting the blockade slowly choking the South.
Still, he was duty bound to listen. In less than two years the U. S.
Navy had effectively closed down every Confederate harbor except

This battered lighthouse
stood at the mouth of
Mobile Bay. Its pock-
marked walls attest to the
intensity of the Union
efforts to seize the important Southern port.

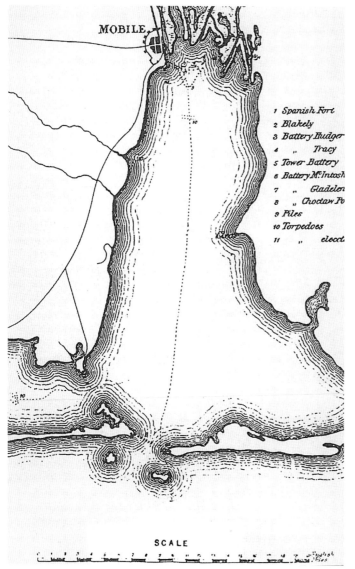

MOBILE

1 Spanish Fort
2 Blakely
3 Battery Hudger
4   „   Tracy
5 Tower Battery
6 Battery McIntosh
7   „   Gladden
8   „   Choctaw Po
9 Files
10 Torpedoes
11 „   elect.

SCALE

In 1863, the *Pioneer II* sank in a storm somewhere along the dotted line running down the center of this map of Mobile Bay.

Mobile; Charleston; Wilmington, North Carolina; and Galveston, Texas.

The admiral observed the *Pioneer's* trial runs in the waters around Mobile over the winter of 1862–63. He was dismayed by the sub's lack of speed; despite the more streamlined profile, the manually powered vessel could only move through the water at about two miles per hour.

Buchanan also was skeptical of its ability to deliver a payload. The original idea was for the *Pioneer II* to tow a torpedo, dive under the targeted ship and, once safely past, detonate the explosive beneath the hull. "I don't think it could be made effective against the enemy off the harbor," he judged, "as the blockading vessels are anchored in water too shallow to permit the boat to pass under."

Nonetheless, one day in early February 1863, it was decided that the *Pioneer II* was ready make an attack on the Federal fleet. The intention was to tow it to Fort Morgan, where it would be fully manned and armed with a torpedo, then launched against an unsuspecting Union warship.

But "the weather was rough," recalled Alexander, "and with a heavy sea the boat became unmanageable." The wildly tossing waves broke across the hatches, which had been left open to provide the crew with fresh air. The submarine filled with water. Despite frantic efforts to bail it out, the swamped vessel finally rolled over and plunged to the floor of Mobile Bay, where it rests in an unknown location to this day. The only positive was that no lives had been lost—a rarity in submarine mishaps.

Informed of the failed mission, Buchanan grumpily assumed an attitude of "I told you so."

The story of submarines during the Civil War wasn't without its romantic subplots. Miss Queenie Bennett of Mobile was the sweetheart of Lieutenant George Dixon, who would captain the *Hunley* the night it sank the *Housatonic*.

"I never entertained but one opinion as to the result of this boat," he said, "that it should prove a failure, and such has been the case."

⸺

To say that Hunley, McClintock, Watson, and Alexander were severely disappointed is to understate matters. But the inventors continued to have their backers. A major supporter was General Dabney Herndon Maury, who four months after the accident was appointed military commander of the District of the Gulf, a position he would hold until war's end. The sawed-off general—dubbed "Ol' Puss in Boots" because he stuffed his short legs into thigh-high boots—was a brave and resourceful officer who had demonstrated his mettle as a young cavalryman in the Mexican War. A graduate of the University of Virginia's law school and West Point, as well as a skillful writer, the forty-one-year-old Maury had an orderly mind and a fertile imagination. The blend allowed him to handle such novel notions as submarine warfare. The fact that his uncle was underwater explosives expert Matthew Fountaine Maury made him even more receptive to the idea.

Another key supporter was E. C. Singer, a gunsmith who had made himself into an authority on underwater explosives. In 1863 Singer and a fellow Texan, Dr. J. R. Fretwell, were manufacturing the Fretwell-Singer torpedo—an underwater contact mine—for the Confederacy. These floating tin cones, partially filled with gunpowder, featured a spring-activated plunger that smashed a percussion cap inside its watertight compartment. Ingenuity was in Singer's blood; a dozen years earlier, his Uncle Isaac had invented the famous continuous-stitch sewing machine bearing his name.

Singer also displayed a certain genius for organization. Along with three fellow members of the Engineering Bureau of the Confederate War Department—Gus Whitney, R. W. Dunn, and J. D. Breaman—he formed an association called the Singer Submarine Corps. The group reached an agreement with the Confederate government that granted members half of the value of any vessel captured or destroyed through the use of its inventions.

With their first submarine deep-sixed and the second beyond the reach of salvage crews, Hunley's consortium would once again have to build from scratch—an expensive proposition. It's not known whether Hunley sought out Singer or it was the other way around. But sometime in the middle of 1863 the two men got

together and ironed out the financial arrangement that would build a third, and final, submarine.

Singer invested $5,000 for a one-third share in Hunley's newest submarine venture. Hunley put up $5,000 himself for another one-third share. He then sold the remaining stock to Whitney, Dunn, and Breaman for $5,000. The total capitalization amounted to $15,000. With financing in place, McClintock, Watson, and Alexander rolled up their sleeves and got back to serious work at the Park and Lyons machine shop.

Years later, Alexander described how the craft that came to be known as the *CSS H. L. Hunley* was fashioned out of a cylinder boiler, forty-eight inches in diameter and twenty-five feet long:

> We cut this boiler in two, longitudinally, and inserted two twelve-inch boiler iron strips in her sides; lengthened her by one tapering course fore and aft, to which were attached bow and stern castings, making the boat about thirty feet long, four feet wide, and 5 feet deep. A longitudinal strip 12 inches wide was

Ironclads were virtually impenetrable, but their low profile and heavy weight made them susceptible to swamping in heavy seas. This contemporary illustration shows the legendary *Monitor* sinking in a gale off the coast of North Carolina on December 31, 1862, while being tugged by the *USS Rhode Island.*

riveted the full length on top. At each end a bulk-head was riveted across to form water-ballast tanks . . . they were used in raising and sinking the boat. In addition to these . . . the boat was ballasted by flat castings, made to fit the outside bottom of the shell and fastened thereto by "Tee" headed bolts passing through stuffing boxes inside the boat, the inside end of [each] bolt squared to fit a wrench, that the bolts might be turned and the ballast dropped, should the necessity arise.

In connection with each of the water tanks there was a sea-cock open to the sea to supply the tank for sinking; also a force pump to eject the water from the tanks in the sea for raising the boat to the surface. There was also a bilge connection to the pump. A mercury gauge, open to the sea, was attached to the shell near the forward tank, to indicate the depth of the boat below the surface. A one and a quarter [inch] shaft passed through the stuffing boxes on each side of the boat, just forward of the end of the propeller shaft. On each end of this shaft, outside the boat . . . fins, five feet long and eight inches wide, were secured. This shaft was operated by a lever amidships, and by raising or lowering the ends of these fins, operated as the fins of a fish, changing the depth of the boat below the surface at will, without disturbing the water level in the ballast tanks.

The rudder was operated by a wheel, and levers connected to rods passing through stuffing boxes in the stern castings, and operated by the captain or pilot forward. An adjusted compass was placed in front of the forward tank. The boat was operated by manual power, with an ordinary propeller. On the propeller shaft there were forward eight cranks at different angles . . . the men sitting on the port side turning on the cranks. The propeller shaft and cranks took up so much room that it was very difficult to pass fore and aft, and when the men were in their places this was next to impossible. In operation, one half of the crew had to pass through the fore hatch, the other through the after hatchway. The propeller revolved in a wrought iron ring or band, to guard against a line being thrown in to foul it.

The two hatchways were sixteen by twelve inches, said Alexander, with a raised frame (called a coaming) eight inches high. The hatches had hinged covers with rubber gaskets and were bolted shut from the inside. In the ends and sides of the coamings, "glasses were inserted to sight from." In effect the coaming acted as a conning tower, its portholes giving the officer in command a view while the sub was partially submerged.

"Damn the torpedoes!" was Admiral David Farragut's famous exhortation at the Battle of Mobile Bay on August 5, 1864. It came at a critical moment in the battle, when Farragut forced his fleet through a minefield that had just claimed the monitor *Tecumseh*. Fort Morgan soon fell, giving control of Mobile Bay to the U. S. Navy.

"There was an opening made in the top of the boat for an air box," Alexander said, "a casting with a close top twelve by eighteen by four inches, made to carry a hollow shaft . . . on the outside was a lever with a stopcock to admit air."

Alexander detailed a typical training exercise.

"All hands aboard and ready, they would fasten the hatch covers down tight, light a candle, then let the water in from the sea into the ballast tanks until the top of the shell was about three inches under water," he wrote. "This could be seen by the water level showing through the glasses in the hatch coamings."

At this point the sea cocks were closed and the submarine put under way.

"The captain would then lower the lever," continued Alexander, "and depress the forward end of the fins very slightly, noting on the mercury gauge the depth of the boat beneath the surface; then bring the fins to a level; the boat would remain and travel at that depth. To rise to a higher level in the water he would raise the lever and elevate the forward end of the fins, and the boat would rise to its original position in the water.

"If the boat was not underway, in order to rise to the surface, it was necessary to start the pumps, and lighten the load by ejecting the water from the tanks onto the sea. In making a landing, the second officer would open his hatch cover, climb out and pass a line to the shore. . . ."

Interestingly, the vessel was not yet known as the *Hunley* but by the rather unwieldy "Whitney's submarine boat," after one of its investors, Gus Whitney. It suggests that at this point Whitney, a respected mechanical engineer, probably had some significant input regarding the design and construction of the boat. At times he also served as first officer, in charge of operating the ballast tanks in the rear of the boat. McClintock typically was in command, stationed in the front and operating the forward diving planes, though another engineer on detached duty from the 21st Alabama, Lieutenant George E. Dixon, also took a regular turn at commanding the vessel.

Hunley was unable to keep as close a watch as he would have liked on the proceedings. Hunley, who held the rank of captain, was frequently out of town on various missions—some undoubtedly clandestine in nature—for the Confederate government. Nonetheless, he maintained an avid interest in all aspects of the boat's construction, regularly corresponding with McClintock and inquiring of its progress and problems.

On July 31, 1863, more than five months after the *Pioneer II* sank, Admiral Buchanan was among a group of high-ranking military men on the shore of the Mobile River to watch the new vessel's mock attack on a moored flat-boat. That morning, nine men—all volunteers—crowded into the craft and bolted the hatches shut from the inside. The boat slipped low into the water until only the top few inches of the coaming, fitted with glass view ports, showed. The men methodically worked the hand crank, the propeller spun, and the boat glided through the murky water, dragging at the end of a 200-foot-long rope one of E. C. Singer's contact mines. As it approached the flatboat the captain took his last compass reading, depressed the diving planes, and lit a candle for illumination as the now fully submerged submarine silently sank into the inky depths. It dropped twenty feet before leveling off.

General Dabney H. Maury, the nephew of Matthew Fountaine Maury, skillfully command-ed the defense of Mobile and was supportive of Horace Hunley's and James McClintock's attempts to build a practical submarine.

With this the knot of observers lost sight of the vessel. There was a period of anxious waiting, some on shore holding their breath even as those on board cranked and sucked the diminishing air supply. The boat had already passed under the flatboat and was out of harm's way when the torpedo exploded with a head-rattling blast. The concussion caused the submariners to rattle around like pebbles inside a tin can, but they immediately recovered and the vessel made the surface with no problem. The men emerged tri-umphantly from the hatches to cheers and applause, a salve for their ringing ears.

The demonstration could hardly have gone better, though Buchanan, for one, had his sense of fair play offended by the lethal exhibition. Like many old salts in both navies, Buchanan had a real distaste for the unconventional weapons modern war had wrought: mines and submarines, all lumped under the disparaging label of "infernal machines." There was something terribly unsettling about sneaking up on the enemy and killing him—"assassination at the bottom of the sea," as da Vinci had termed it. But the admiral also owed his allegience to his country, and in the summer of 1863 the Confederacy was being strangled as surely as if Lincoln himself had a grip on Jefferson Davis's windpipe.

The very next day, Buchanan wrote Captain John Tucker, recently placed in charge of the Confederate naval squadron defending Charleston.

> Sir: Yesterday I witnessed the destruction of a lighter or coal flat in the Mobile River by a torpedo which was placed under it by a submarine iron boat, the invention of Messrs. Whitney and McClintock; Messrs. Watson and Whitney visit Charleston for the purpose of consulting General Beauregard and yourself to ascertain whether you will try it, they will explain all its advantages, and if it can operate in smooth water where the current is not so strong as was the case yesterday. I can recommend it to your favorable consideration, it can be propelled about four knots per hour, to judge from the experiment of yesterday. I am fully satisfied it can be used successfully in blowing up one or more of the enemy's ironclads in your harbor. Do me the favor to show this to General Beauregard with my regards.

In Charleston, General P. G. T. Beauregard read the letter with great interest. He immediately called for an interview with Watson and Whitney. After looking over their drawings and listening to their plans, he wasted no time in sending for the secret weapon that had so impressed Admiral Buchanan.

On August 7, Beauregard telegraphed railroad authorities. "Please expedite transportation of Whitney's submarine boat from Mobile here," he commanded, "it is much needed."

BEAUREGARD:

The Napoleon of the Confederacy

Pierre Gustave Toutant Beauregard. It was a name that delighted Southern society as so charmingly and elegantly French. Actually, the surnames were at one time joined by a hyphen until the bearer separated them and adopted the latter for brevity. His fellow Creoles had a way of shortening it still further, pronouncing the name "Beau-gar." As for the first name, the general preferred Gustave, though early in the Civil War he was dubbed "Felix," a Roman name meaning "favored by the gods."

Born on May 28, 1818, Beauregard grew up speaking French. His family—descended from immigrants to Louisiana when it was part of the domain of King Louis XIV—owned extensive lands outside New Orleans and was one of the major sugar cane producers in the region. When he was eleven he went to New York City to study at a prep school operated by two of Napoleon's former officers. Under their influence the boy cultivated a desire for a military career and, not surprisingly, a lifelong fascination with the warrior emperor of France, Napoleon Bonaparte. (Years later, he would inject such Napoleonic maxims as "le secret de la guerre est dans la sureté des communica-tions" in his military correspondence.)

Beauregard never hesitated to use favors and influence to get what he wanted. Hungry for a martial education, he used his father's political connections to get a Congressional appointment to West Point when he was sixteen. As one of the youngest plebes ever admitted, he excelled at classwork and in forming associations. His classmates included several who would gain fame in the Civil War, including future commanders Jubal Early, Braxton Bragg, Joseph Hooker, and William T. Sherman.

Beauregard graduated second in his class and was rewarded with a commission in the Corps of Engineers. In that era, when a need was perceived for protection against foreign invasion, he showed strong construction talent and was placed in charge of building permanent fortifications along the Mississippi River. During the

Beauregard as a young officer.

Judah P.
Benjamin grew up in
Charleston and was a
Louisiana senator
before becoming secre-
tary of war for the
Confederacy.

Mexican War he distinguished himself by helping to clear the way to Mexico City. Officers who did well were rewarded with brevet promotions. Beauregard, who was wounded twice, received two of them, but characteristically complained long and hard to his superiors that they were insufficient compensation.

After the war Beauregard returned to Louisiana and the building of government works. He also patented some river navigation aids and a quirky artillery carriage. In 1850, his wife of nine years—Maire Laure Villere, the stunningly beautiful daughter of a prosperous Creole—died of complications following the birth of their third child and only daughter. He would marry again in 1860, this time to Caroline Deslonde, the plain-looking daughter of another Creole plantation owner.

By then Beauregard was a captain in the regular army and supervising the repair and expansion of the custom house in New Orleans. In early 1861, due to the influence of his new wife's brother-in-law, John Slidell (an influential Louisiana politician who would gain notoriety as one of two Confederate diplomats seized in the "Trent Affair"), he was appointed superintendent of the U. S. Military Academy.

Beauregard's tenure was the shortest in West Point history: five days. This was the time of the great "secession crisis," when all Southerners in government service could be suspected of delivering men or material to the fledgling Confederate government. After appointing Beauregard superintendent, John B. Floyd, a Virginian, left his post as U. S. Secretary of War. His replacement wasted no time in rescinding Beauregard's appointment.

His lofty sense of honor offended, Beauregard resigned his commission and offered his services to the Confederate cause. Newly elected President Jefferson Davis appointed him a brigadier general, an extraordinary jump in rank for an officer who had not achieved field grade in the peacetime U. S. Army.

Beauregard's first assignment appealed to his ego as well as to his natural engineering talent: if the Federal government refused to abandon Fort Sumter outside Charleston, he was to take it and secure the harbor for his country.

Charleston aristocracy embraced the cultivated Creole. The social demands made on the energetic, nervous commander—then approaching forty-three years of age—threatened to distract him from his official duties. Said one member of Charleston society: "Beauregard is a demigod here to most of the natives."

The striking Beauregard stood out among other Southerners in their new tailored gray uniforms. Most distinctive was his complexion. It was "brunette, sallow, and the sun and wind had made it resemble bronze," recalled one cavalry officer. His eyes were "large, dark, melancholy, with the lids drooping and somewhat inflamed by long vigils—of a peculiar dreamy expression—those eyes impressed the beholder very strangely. It was the eye of the bloodhound with his fighting instincts asleep, but ready at any moment to be strung for action." A broad brow, firm mouth covered with a heavy black mustache and protruding chin gave his countenance, in this officer's view, "that of a French marshal of the empire." Beauregard would have loved that comparison.

Although concerned about his appearance, the only thing jaunty about Beauregard was the French kepi he favored. A serious, unsmiling man, there was little that was gay or funloving about him. In fact, he possessed a brooding temperament.

Fort Sumter fell on April 14, 1861, after thirty-four hours of shelling. The affair was brief and remarkably unbloody, but war fever was so hot in the South that Beauregard's success was elevated to something akin to the taking of Gibraltar.

Declared the "hero of Sumter," he was summoned to Richmond to head one of two forces being readied to repel an expected Yankee invasion of northern Virginia. The Richmond public clamored for a look at him. Then, satisfied with what they saw, the people sent him off to the war's first large battle.

It came in July 1861 at Mansassas, Virginia, long before either side was ready for such a meeting. The Battle of Manassas (known as Bull Run in the North) was an unsophisticated clash of two undisciplined crowds of inexperienced men, a fight that proved to be a chaotic affair in which units performed virtually out of the control of the commanding generals. But the result was what mattered. And once again Beauregard—who had a horse killed under him while trying to lead one 20,000-man wing of the Confederate army—was singled out and acclaimed for the Southern victory. The fact that Brigadier General Joseph E. Johnston actually held full command on the field was ignored. Richmond was almost agog with "old Bory."

President Davis promoted him to full general while admirers named babies, cakes, and ladies garments after him. Atrocious poems appeared in the press: "Oh, the north was evil-starred, when she met thee,

Jefferson Davis.

Beauregard!" Women showered him with romantic letters and flowers and besieged him for photographs and buttons from his tunic.

As pleasant as all this celebrity was for a man with Beauregard's vanity, it cannot be said that he handled it well. He came into conflict with Davis's most trusted cabinet member, Secretary of War Judah Benjamin. After Benjamin forbade Beauregard to recruit a rocket battery company on the technical grounds that it was without "warrant in law" for him to raise such a unit, the thin-skinned general wrote a scathing denunciation of this "functionary at his desk" to Davis.

For his part, Davis was wary of Beauregard's immense popularity, which could in the future pose a threat to his presidency. Beauregard had already demonstrated an interest in politics, having previously run unsuccessfully for mayor of New Orleans.

What altered Beauregard's relationship forever with Davis was the president's alleged rejection of an ambitious plan to capture Baltimore and Washington, which embarrassed him when it appeared in several Southern newspapers in October 1861.

The plan in question was only the first in a long series of strategic proposals Beauregard advanced during the war. Each was rejected and almost always for the same basic reasons: all seemed too complex and involved closely coordinated movements that defied the realities of logisitics and available resources. Moreover, they lacked an appreciation of the Confederate government's broader concerns and objectives.

With both Davis and Benjamin angry with him, Beauregard was "doubly doomed," said one observer. He was sent far away from Richmond, to the Western theatre. There he enjoyed uneven success protecting Confederate positions along the Mississippi River, some of which he had designed years before. Then he marched his men to Corinth, Mississippi, and joined them to the force of General Albert S. Johnston.

Johnston held overall command of the western forces and planned to move on Major General U. S. Grant's army in southwest Tennessee in early April 1862. The attack came at Pittsburgh Landing, Tennessee, a fight remembered in history as the Battle of Shiloh. When Johnston was mortally wounded, Beauregard had to take command and continue the attack. He launched one ferocious assault after another on the Federals' last-ditch positions but could not overrun them. Ultimately, he disengaged his army, pulled it back to Corinth, and remained in a defensive position through the end of May before marching them to Tupelo in northeast Mississippi.

Controversy and complaints rained down on Beauregard. He

was criticized for not capitalizing on the early gains his men had made on the Shiloh battlefield. His withdrawal to Tupelo, while not once engaging the enemy, further aggravated Richmond authorities. "I fear he has been placed too high for his mental strength," Davis confided to his wife, "as he does not exhibit the ability manifested on smaller fields."

Beauregard, his health broken by the campaign, then decided to take a leave of absence in Alabama. He left his command to General Braxton Bragg without first waiting for authorization, a move that gave the furious Davis the rationale for relieving Beauregard permanently of his command.

Beauregard was beside himself—particularly for having given Davis an excuse, however flimsy, to move against him. He bitterly wrote a friend: "My consolation is, that the difference between 'that individual' and myself is that, if he were to die today, the whole country would rejoice at it, whereas, I believe, if the same thing were to happen to me, they would regret it."

When Beauregard was sufficiently recovered to return to duty, the War Department assigned him to head the Department of South Carolina and Georgia, with headquarters at Charleston.

Beauregard held his Carolinas post for eighteen months, longer than any of his other Civil War assignments. It was his most effective posting. There, he was responsible for protecting the South Carolina, Georgia, and Florida coast and for keeping such ports as Charleston and Savannah open. By carefully maneuvering and redeploying a force that never exceeded 20,000 men, and by using his engineering skill to strengthen Fort Sumter and the other installations in his department, he was able to resist successive Union assaults by land and sea.

For his labors, Beauregard probably received more credit in the Northern press than he did from his own superiors. The April 24, 1863, issue of the *New York World* opined:

One result of the Charleston fight will be to restore Beauregard to favor of the Southern people. Truly he is boastful, egotistical, untruthful, and wanting in tact, but he is certainly the most marvelous engineer of modern times. By his genius and professional skill he has erected batteries in Charleston harbor that would sink all the wooden fleets of the world did they come under fire, and he has succeeded, moreover, in driving back in disgrace the most impenetrable ironclad fleet afloat. There is no denying what the man has done, unpalatable though it may be to the Northern people.

Among innovations adapted at Charleston was a light-draught torpedo ram to be used against ironclads; his tactical response to the Federal blockade was to organize boarding parties, armed with revolvers, to attack the Union gunboats at night. These activities kept the city's spirit high and its citizens involved. But while he was very much at home in Charleston and admired by its people, he was not happy there. He felt passed over, on the shelf. He complained in a letter: "You are, no doubt, aware that not those officers who stand the highest in the estimation of the War Department are sent here permanently. In fact, this has been called 'the Department of Refuge.'"

The feud between Beauregard and his detractors in Richmond continued throughout the rest of the war, though Beauregard never neglected his duty to his country. Given to dark moods, his energy noticeably waned as he remained

General Beauregard (on horse) directs the building of fortifications on James Island in 1863.

away from the primary war theaters. The famous Charleston diarist, Mary Chestnut, noted, "of late they say he has fallen into a green sickness—melancholia." To a close friend, the general confided that Davis had "done more than if he had thrust a fratricidal dagger into my heart! He has killed my enthusiasm in our holy cause."

Then, to add to his misery, in spring 1864 he lost his second wife, who had spent the entire war ill in New Orleans. That April he

was recalled to Virginia. There he assisted a strong admirer, General Robert E. Lee, whom he had served with during the Mexican War, in defending the southern approaches to Richmond. A new assignment soon took him to Georgia, where he was put in titular command of the ragtag forces thrown together to stop Sherman's march to the sea in 1864–65.

Beauregard's war ended in Greensboro, North Carolina. After Richmond's fall, Davis and his cabinet fled there in the spring of 1865. Beauregard was asked for his advice on how to save the disintegrating nation. The general, his plans so often rejected in the past by Davis, could only concur with others that all was lost.

The war over, Beauregard returned to an empty house in New Orleans with one silver dollar in his pocket, the mustering out pay he and his staff took from the Confederate Treasury. Like many other professional soldiers who served the Lost Cause, he found himself deprived of his livelihood. And like others he thought of going abroad as a soldier of fortune. Over the next several years there were periodic negotiations with the governments of Brazil, Spain, Egypt, and France. But his thoughts of expatriation were forgotten when an opportunity arose that called for both his engineering talent and administrative skill: assuming the presidency of the New Orleans, Jackson & Mississippi Railway.

His reputation suffered, however, when after five years of railroading he left to become a commissioner of the notoriously corrupt Louisiana Lottery. The job came with a salary approaching $30,000 a year, a sum considered astronomical at the time—especially in the economically depressed South.

For nearly twelve years, Beauregard went through the debasing exercise of drawing and reading off to assembled hopefuls the winning ticket numbers and the prize amounts, lending by his white hair, dignified manner and credentials as a high-ranking Confederate general an air of respectability to the charade.

Beauregard stayed active in veterans affairs. When John Bell Hood and his wife died in a yellow fever epidemic that swept New Orleans in 1879, he arranged to have the late general's memoirs published and its proceeds given over to the support of their ten surviving children.

When Beauregard decided to tell his own story, he employed the writing skills of his former aide, Alfred Roman. The result was a massive two-volume work published under Roman's name. But it was in reality an autobiography, so closely did the subject control its contents. This allowed the inclusion of considerable praise that would have seemed uncomely had Beauregard's name been affixed as author. The text at no point acknowledged any mistakes Beauregard may have made in the course of the war. Those readers not privy to the political in-fighting, the intrigues, and the difficult aspects of the general's personality or the limitations of his military intellect, were left wondering why this man whom victory seemed so often to favor was not better utilized in the war.

As Napoleon warned, the ambitious Beauregard did make mistakes, though few were on the battlefield, where he was sublimely confident and competent. It was between the engagements, when he began to think as the Emperor and create grand strategies, when he began to tactlessly criticize his superiors, annoying those in power and making them wary and uneasy about him, that Beauregard did himself in. Had he handled affairs differently, a higher place in Confederate history might have been his.

But, as it stood, when he died in 1893 in New Orleans at age seventy-five, Beauregard was a comfortable, wealthy gentleman, a fellow who, unlike so many other Southern career soldiers, took up the role civilian life had assigned him and played it well. He became the man with the marvelous name and white coif, the man who called the lottery numbers.

—*Gerard Patterson*

General P. G. T. Beauregard, military commander of Charleston.

Chapter Three

THE MURDERING MACHINE

General Pierre Gustave Toutant Beauregard, a product of the Creole planter aristocracy of New Orleans, was ambitious, temperamental, and as vain as a peacock. Southern belles regularly sent him bouquets of flowers, to which he was known to respond with an unsolicited photograph of himself tucked inside the thank you note. Admirers observed that his once gleaming dark hair was rapidly turning gray and attributed it to the pressures of commanding the defense of Charleston. The general's young Spanish valet and barber knew better; because of the blockade, the availability of certain toilet articles, including hair dye, had dried up.

For all of his vanities, the forty-five-year-old general also was a genuine Southern hero and first-rate engineer with a demonstrated interest in innovation. As a young army officer in the 1850s, he had filed several patents and advocated an exotic cure for hydrophobia. As commander of the Carolina and Georgia coastal defenses, he had skillfully woven in the use of novel weapons like torpedoes and armored rams to frustrate the enemy. Now he was calling on the services of another infernal machine, that of the Singer Submarine Corps.

The North regarded Charleston as the "hornet's nest of

sedition." The Ordinance of Secession had been signed there, and it was the site of the first Federal defeat of the war—the taking of Fort Sumter by Beauregard's batteries. According to one U. S. admiral, "no city in the South was so obnoxious to Union men as Charleston. Richmond was the objective point of our armies, as its capture was expected to end the war, but it excited little sentiment and little antipathy. It was to . . . Charleston that the strong feeling of dislike was directed, and the desire was general to punish that city by all the rigors of war." The siege of Charleston would wind up being the longest campaign of the war, lasting from the first failed assault in 1862 until the city finally capitulated three years later.

Thanks in large part to Beauregard's preparations, by the spring of 1863 Charleston was being described with grudging admiration as "almost the strongest place by sea in the world" by Union naval officers. The city sat on a narrow peninsula between two rivers, the Ashley and Cooper, about seven miles from the bar that stretched across the mile-and-a-half-wide mouth of the harbor. Charleston harbor was defended by several forts and batteries on Sullivan's Island to the north and Morris Island and James Island to the south, forming an interlocking "circle of fire" that was anchored by Fort Sumter.

In the summer of 1863, the situation had grown desperate for the stalwart Confederate defenders. Charleston was under the gun like no place before and few since. During one week-long, round-the-clock bombardment in July, for example, Union shore batteries and warships pounded Fort Sumter with 5,643 shells, an average of one every two minutes. The masonry walls sagged into shapeless heaps. But still the terrified garrison hung on, enduring the whistling shot and shell with courage and grim good humor.

The intensity of the Charleston campaign was encapsulated in the Union land assault on Fort Wagner on July 18, 1863. The earthen redoubt at the northern end of Morris Island held great strategic importance. Capturing it would allow the Federals to move a battery within a mile and a half of Fort Sumter's crumbling walls and provide a launching pad for a major offensive against Charleston.

The furious head-on assault on Fort Wagner was immortalized in the 1989 film, *Glory*. Hollywood's depiction of the carnage inflicted on the attackers, including the Negro troops of the 54th Massachusetts, was not nearly as graphic as it could have been. The Union lost more than 1,500 men in a matter of hours. Many were

A shell explodes inside the city of Charleston. Union siege guns occasionally lobbed shells into the city as a way of terrorizing the civilian population.

blown apart by artillery fire or were drowned overnight by the incoming tide. Gulls, crabs, and rats picked at the headless torsos and shattered limbs that were scattered over the sandy beach and blood-splattered parapets. "I never saw such a sight as presented itself on Sunday morning at day break," wrote one Confederate soldier to his family in Georgia:

> [As] far as the eye could reach could be seen the dead and dying on all sides could be seen the result of the fight. I volentered to go out to collect the wounded yankees. I had a chance to see what was to be seen—in the ditch to our left there was 115 killed in a space of about 100 feet—So you can see that there was some brave yankees engaged—I never saw such a sight, men with heads off many with legs shot off—feet, hands and in fact any part of the body—Such complete destruction of life—So wholesale—it makes me shudder to think about it. One poor fellow I saw had a [cannon] ball shot through his head taking off the forhead both eyes and his ear—I would like to forget his appearance he was alive twenty-four hours after the fight—others so shot as to be unable to tell if man or beast—the killed was about 8 to 1 wounded generaly it is just the revirse.

On August 12 the submarine arrived in war-weary Charleston. It was cradled and tied fast to two flatcars, and undoubtedly hidden beneath tarps. A growing crowd of curious Charlestonians watched as the bulky, odd-looking craft was carefully unloaded and then slowly moved from the railroad station to a nearby dock on

Southern soldier-artist Conrad Wise Chapman painted this placid view of Charleston's harbor, with Union iron-clads in the foreground and Charleston in the background. At the right is Castle Pinckney, which like all harbor forts was under constant bombardment throughout the war.

These picture cards of the Union batteries on Morris Island were made by the obscure photographic firm of Haas & Peale. The heavy Parrott rifles depicted here were capable of hurling shells 4,300 yards against Fort Sumter's crumbling walls.

the Cooper River. Onlookers doffed their caps, waved flags, and cheered as the boat was rolled through Charleston's streets. Beauregard, equally excited over its presence, instructed the chief quartermaster and the arsenal commander to furnish Whitney, Watson, and the rest of the band from Mobile whatever they needed to place their vessel in service.

Desperation was in the air. George Alfred Trenholm was a senior partner in the blue-chip exporting firm of John Fraser & Company, which had a contract with the Confederate government to smuggle in war supplies. The profits from blockade running, an activity that was slowed but never stopped in Charleston, made the already wealthy Trenholm fabulously rich. So rich that the dashing Trenholm (who many believe was the model for the Rhett Butler character in Margaret Mitchell's 1936 novel, *Gone with the Wind*) was able to make an amazing offer just as the submarine and its crew arrived in Charleston. General Thomas Jordan, Beauregard's chief of staff, forwarded the message:

> I am authorized to say that John Fraser & Co. will pay over to any parties who shall destroy the US Steam ironclad "Ironside" the sum of $100,000, a similar sum for the destruction of the wooden frigate "Wabash," and the sum of $50,000 for every monitor sunk. I have reason to believe that other men of wealth will unite and give with equal munificence toward the same end. At the same time steps are being taken to secure a large sum to be settled for the support of the families of parties, who, making any attempt against the fleet now attacking our outer works, shall fail in the enterprise, and fall or be captured in the attempt.

General Thomas Lanier Clingman was the commander of Sullivan's Island when the *Hunley* was moved from Mobile to Charleston in mid-August 1863. Known for his impatience and unbending viewpoints, Clingman almost immediately judged the submarine's civilian management team to be ineffective and timid, resulting in the boat being seized by military authorities less than two weeks after its arrival.

In the minds of the local military authorities, the bounty, coupled with the submariners' expressed desire to serve the Confederate cause, should have had the adventurers from Mobile flying to get into the fray. First, though, they had to become acclimated to their new surroundings. A base was established in a cove behind Fort Moultrie on the southern end of Sullivan's Island.

While the vessel was being readied for what Beauregard assumed would be a quick, bold strike at the Union fleet, Horace Hunley was away on another government mission, this time in Mississippi. "I have been extremely anxious about your experiments in Charleston," he wrote McClintock at his Charleston hotel.

"It is not at all on the question of whether you will succeed in blowing up a vessel of the enemy, for I think that more than probable and of itself only a small matter. It is whether your success will be made available in effecting a real solid benefit to the Confederacy and conferring glory on its originators.

"I am anxious first and above all for a dead silence on your part that the enemy may be lost in uncertainty and mystery, which is more dreadful than any understood evil even of the greatest magnitude. Secondly, while in a panic if you succeed the enemy, if properly pressed before he can make preparations to resist the consequences of your success, might be possibly driven entirely from Morris Island, his works destroyed and guns spiked even if it be not

"Chicora"

The rebel ironclad *Chicora* distinguished itself during the siege of Charleston. Its only losses during the entire war was when several crew members volunteered for duty aboard the *Hunley*.

possible to take and permanently hold the island. . . . Therefore, as I cannot join you I would be glad to have you in conversation with General Beauregard if this reaches you before your experiment to ask him (by way of suggestion) if you should be so fortunate as to succeed, and if that success should create a panic and consequent retreat, if a rapid descent by vessels and men could not drive the enemy from the island.

"If he should think that a panic and retreat of the enemies could effect such a result, then make every effort first to get him to prepare silently for such an event, and then by at least one spare torpedo for a second attempt make a heroic attempt to produce this panic. Remind your crew of Manassas and Shiloh and the consequences of faltering in the hour of success and make one grand effort. . . . [Y]ou may have cause to rejoice over the fruits of your labor and that like men in more exalted positions, you did not stop to rejoice over your small gains [and] let slip a vast success and immortal honor. Read this to Whitney."

Hunley came to Charleston on August 20, anxious to prove his and his men's worth—no more anxious than the military authorities, it developed. After the massacre at Fort Wagner, the Union forces under Major General Quincy Adams Gillmore settled in for a long season of seige. Gillmore, a young, brilliant engineer who had finished first in his class at West Point fourteen years earlier, had secured his reputation with the successful bombardment and capture of Fort Pulaski, Georgia, where his rifled guns had reduced the masonry fortifications to rubble. Now he proposed to do the same here. Trenches were built that put long-range Parrott rifles within reach of not only Fort Wagner, but Fort Sumter as well. On August 17, another devastating bombardment of Sumter began. Over the next week the Parrott guns, supported by ironclads, together hurled 6,800 rounds at it. The ragged, hollow-eyed men inside lived like moles, burrowing into the rubble during the day and then emerging at night to make whatever repairs they could.

On August 21, Beauregard received a message from Gillmore. He demanded the evacuation of Fort Sumter and Morris Island within four hours. Otherwise, he warned, "I shall open fire on the city of Charleston."

General Quincy Adams Gillmore.

Beauregard was outraged. He furiously penned a reply to Gillmore: "Among nations not barbarous the usage of war prescribes that when a city is about to be attacked, timely notice shall be given by the attacking commander, in order that noncombatants may have an opportunity for withdrawing beyond its limits. . . . It would appear, sir, that despairing of reducing these works, you now resort to the novel measure of turning your guns against the old men, the women and children, and the hospitals of a sleeping city, an act of inexcusable barbarity."

Gillmore was unmoved by Beauregard's invocation of civilized warfare. That night heavy shells began falling on Charleston. Businessman C. R. Burckmyer survived the shelling to record his experiences in a letter to his wife:

> Sunday night I went to bed at eleven and was waked up at twelve by a terrific noise and loud cries in the street. I jumped up and found a crowd before

our door who were evidently in a great state of excitement. I rushed into the piazza and found old Jane in her night dress hanging out of her window. She cried to me "O Master, something fell on the shed and has broken in the ceiling." I immediately concluded that it was a shell and hurried to wake Edwin. He was so soundly asleep however, that not having a light I thought at first that he had been struck by the shell and had become a victim to Yankee malignity and hate.

I succeeded in waking him at last and together we went out into the street to investigate matters. We found that a shell had entered the house directly opposite to us, formerly occupied by Mrs. Meyers, and commencing at the back garret had descended to the side walk through the house, passing through both floors and penetrating the walls as though they were paste board. Fortunately no one was hurt, although the house was badly damaged.

Our door steps were crowded with brick and mortar and some of the bricks from the opposite house broke away a portion of our carriage gate. While we were in the street examining and looking around we heard another shell coming which broke just over the Artesian Well and then another which fell in Chapin's carriage yard. Here a cry was raised in the crowd that the Yankees had the range of that block and that it was no longer safe. No sooner said than the crowd scattered and in two minutes not a soul was left in the lately crowded street.

Gillmore's weapon of terror was a large Parrott gun mounted on a platform in a Morris Island marsh. Before its barrel burst, the "Swamp Angel" sent dozens of 200-pound shells, some filled with an incendiary called Greek fire, crashing into waterfront neighborhoods. Many citizens fled to the upper part of town or to the countryside; others decided to stick it out, tubs of water at the ready.

By the end of their first week in Charleston the submariners from Mobile had gone out on several nocturnal missions, each time returning without result. They would leave the cove behind Fort Moultrie and, wary of the mines, nets, pilings and other obstructions that filled the harbor, hug the coast of Sullivan's Island until they reached open sea. There the Union fleet loomed, impressive in its size and variety: monitors, steam sloops, gunboats, and the daunting broadside ironclad, *New Ironsides*. For whatever rea-

Defending Charleston. These artillerists posed at Fort Pemberton on James Island in 1863.

son—an unfavorable current, poor weather, jitters—on no occasion did McClintock attempt an attack.

On August 23, General Thomas L. Clingman, the harried commander of Sullivan's Island, openly complained in a pair of notes to his aide, Captain William F. Nance. The first read: "The torpedo boat started at sunset but returned as they state because of an accident. Whitney says that though McClintock is timid, yet it shall go tonight unless the weather is bad." This was followed by a more damning message: "The torpedo boat has not gone out. I do not think it will render any service under its present management."

The dawdling exacerbated the already strained patience of Beauregard, who believed that the city's fate might be hanging in the balance. Rightly or wrongly, Beauregard suspected that McClintock and his crew lacked sufficient martial ardor for the task at hand. Practically by definition alone, submariners have always been an unquestionably brave breed. But the newcomers were, both figuratively and literally, in over their heads. Nothing in the comparatively placid waters of Mobile harbor had prepared any of them for the hell-roaring spectacle that was Charleston in August 1863.

RECOLLECTIONS OF CHARLESTON UNDER SEIGE

Colonel Charles H. Olmstead commanded the First Georgia Infantry at Fort Wagner and, after its fall, at Fort Johnson. Both garrisons endured constant and severe battering while protecting Charleston from the Union fleet. After the war Olmstead described his experiences, including his passing acquaintance with the curious craft he referred to as the "Cigar Boat."

Failing in the direct attack, the enemy's endeavor seemed to be to make our berth uncomfortably warm, and here the success was undoubted. Day after day the monitors—some four or five in number—and that tremendous war vessel, the *New Ironsides*, would take their positions directly opposite the fort, at a distance of six to eight hundred yards, the wooden ships being at much longer range. Then would be poured in upon us a steady steam of shot and shell, much more pleasant to dwell upon as a memory than it was to endure, while upon the land side new batteries were

Colonel Charles Olmstead.

built by the enemy, and each day the weight of metal thrown against us would seem to be heavier than the day before.

I well remember the approach of the first monitor. How deliberate its movements; how insignificant its appearance; the deck almost level with the water, and the little black turret giving small promise of its hidden power for attack. My curiosity about the vessel was great, but was soon to be satisfied without stint. There was a slow revolving motion of the turret, a cloud of smoke, a deafening roar, and then, with the rush and noise of an express train, the huge fifteen-inch shell, visible at every point of its trajectory, passed overhead and burst far in the rear. The next shell exploded in the parapet, covering several of us with dirt. The introduction was complete. Thenceforward we held these singular looking craft in wholesome respect. The *Ironsides*, however, was probably the most formidable ship of the fleet. She is said to have carried at bow and stern two-hundred-pound Parrott guns, and nine eleven-inch Dahlgrens on a side. Her broadsides were not fired in volley, but gun after gun, in rapid succession, the effect upon those who were at the wrong end of the guns being exceedingly demoraliz-

ing. Whenever she commenced there was a painful uncertainly as to what might happen before she got through.

We had but one gun with which to fight the monitors—the ten-inch Columbiad located just over the sally port. True, the thirty-twos were tried for a while, but they were so impotent to harm the heavy mail of the ships that their use was soon discontinued. This Columbiad was manned, I think, by the Matthew's Artillery, of South Carolina, and the gunner, Frazer Matthews, was as noble a soldier as the siege produced. In the midst of the hottest fire he would stand quietly on the chassis directing the aiming of the gun with all the coolness and precision of target practice. Never flurried, always intent upon the work before him, and never giving the signal to fire until the aim was

taken to his entire satisfaction, the accuracy of his marksmanship was great. Again and again I saw the solid ten-inch shot strike upon the sides of the monitors, only to break into a thousand fragments, that would splash into the sea like so much grapeshot.

At first we thought that no harm was done by our fire, but we learned afterwards the concussion within the turret was tremendous, and that, among others, one very prominent officer had been killed by it. . . .

Such continuous cannonading, of course, seriously impaired the integrity of our parapets. But as at that stage of the siege the firing ceased at nightfall, opportunity was given to repair damages, and all night long the garrison would work, filling sand bags and painfully endeavoring to make good the yawning chasms and

Fort Sumter is fired upon by the *New Ironsides* and two smaller monitors.

The battered interior of
Fort Sumter in 1863.

ragged craters left by the terrible
missiles that had been hurled into
the fort during the day. There was
a constant strain upon all the fac-
ulties, that gave little time for anything save the stern duties of the
hour, and yet there were humorous
incidents ever occurring that even
now will bring smiles to the lips of
all who remember them.

Who can forget "Aquarius,"
the water bearer, as he was
dubbed—a simple-hearted fellow,
from the backwoods of South
Carolina, who devoted his time to
bringing water to the wounded.
Both heels of his shoes were carried away by a shell, and from
that time he went barefooted—
there was "danger in shoes," he
said. And, then, the simple manner
in which, on returning from one of
his trips to the well he held up one
full jug and only the handle of
another, saying, apologetically,
"Oh, a shell took hit."

I can see in my mind's eye,
too, the brilliant engineering feat
of a member of the Oglethorpe
Light Infantry, who while cooking
a little dinner in the open parade,
provided protection for himself by
placing an empty flour barrel
alongside of the fire, and gravely
sticking his head into it whenever
the scream of a shell warned him
of approaching trouble. . . .

The discomforts and priva-
tions to which the garrison was
subjected rapidly increased, and
soon attained proportions that will
be remembered by those who
endured them, like the details of
some horrible dream. To avoid an
unnecessary loss of life, the men
were kept as much as possible
within the bomb proofs during the
daytime; but the gun squads and
riflemen, of course, were constant-
ly exposed as well as numbers who
could find no room in the shelters,
or who preferred taking the fresh
air, with all its attendant hazards.
From these there were constant

additions to the list of our losses. The wounded (and the wounds were mostly of a terrible character), were all brought in among the men, and the surgical operations were performed in the midst of the crowd, by the light of candles, that dimly burned in the heavy air from which all vitality had been drawn. The cries of these poor sufferers, the unceasing roar of artillery above and around, the loss of rest, the want of pure air, and the baking heat of a Southern summer, all combined to render the position almost unbearable. The enemy's dead from the two assaults had been buried immediately in front of the moat; those from our garrison just back of the fort. From the description of the island it will be understood that shallow graves only could be given—graves from which a high wind would blow the light, sandy soil, or which a bursting shell would rend, exposing the bodies to the sunshine. The whole air was tainted with corruption, and finally the little wells, from which our supply of water was drawn, became so foul, from the same cause, that their use was abandoned, and thenceforward drinking water was sent from the city of Charleston.

Now began a most remarkable feature of the siege, and one that has marked a new era in the science of attack and imposed new and startling problems upon the military engineer charged with the construction of permanent

A tattered Confederate flag flies defiantly at Fort Sumter, in this painting by Conrad Wise Chapman. The stars and stripes wouldn't be run up the flagpole until April 14, 1865, exactly four years to the day that the Federal fort fell.

The *Hunley* as the "cigar boat" would have appeared to Colonel Olmstead. This is the only known photograph of the submarine and was reportedly taken by George Cook in December 1863. The figure at right evidently was later painted in to add a sense of scale or an element of human interest.

fortifications. I allude, of course, to the battering down of the walls of Fort Sumter from a distance of two and a half miles. The power of rifled guns against masonry had been conclusively demonstrated during the previous year at Fort Pulaski. There, however, the breaching batteries were distant about one mile, but there were few who could believe that at more than twice that range Sumter was seriously endangered. It had been thought that the grand old fort was safe so long as Wagner held out. But one morning a new battery opened; the shot and shell went high above our heads, and were hurled with irresistible power against the walls of Sumter. Great masses of masonry from the outer wall fell as each shot struck, and ere many days it seemed as though nought but a pile of ruins would mark the spot.

Here, however, General Beauregard gave splendid evidence of his readiness to meet emergencies, and of his skill as an engineer. As soon as it became evident that

the fort must yield to the power of the heavy artillery brought to bear upon it, he rapidly withdrew all the guns that could be utilized for defensive purpose at other points, and from the very ruins of Sumter, constructed, as it were, a new fortification, fully adequate to the purpose of commanding the ship channel to the city. But all other power of the fort was gone, and in the subsequent events on Morris Island, Sumter took no part. This bombardment lasted for seven days, and in that time a first-class masonry fort was reduced to a shapeless ruin from batteries located at points far beyond the remotest distance at which any engineer had ever dreamed of danger. The debris of the walls fell in a natural slope and served as an impenetrable protection to the lower casemates of the channel face, in which the new battery was placed. Some little time elapsed, however, before these changes were completed and I am unable to understand why Admiral Dahlgren did not meanwhile avail himself of the opening thus offered and push with his ironclads for the inner harbor. We certainly looked for such a dash, and General Gilmore was evidently chagrined at the fact that it was not made. Whether or not such a course would have been successful is problematical. There can be no doubt, through, that it would have added grave complications to the Confederate military position, to say the least of it. . . .

A most interesting feature in this summer's [1863's] operations was the development of the attacking power of moveable torpedoes. Special interest attached to a boat that was brought from Mobile, by railroad, and which was generally known, from its shape, as the "Cigar Boat." Its history is linked with deeds of the loftiest heroism and devotion of self to the service of country. . . .

This boat was one day made fast to the wharf at Fort Johnson, preparatory to an expediiton against the fleet, and taking advantage of the opportunity, I examined it critically. It was built of boiler iron, about thirty feet in length, with a breadth of beam of four feet by a vertical depth of six feet, the figures being approximate only. Access to the interior was had by two man-holes in the upper part, covered by hinged caps, into which were let bull's eyes of heavy glass, and through these the steersman looked in guiding the motions of the craft. The boat floated with these caps raised only a foot or so above the level of the water. The motive power was a propeller, to be worked by hand of the crew, cranks being provided in the shaft for that purpose.

Upon each side of the exterior were horizontal vanes, or wings, that could be adjusted at any angle from the interior. When it was intended that the boat should go on an even keel whether on the surface or under, these vanes were kept level. If it was desired to go below the water, say, for instance, at an angle of ten degrees, the vanes were fixed at that angle, and the propeller worked. The resistance of the water against the vanes would then carry the boat under. A reversal of this method would bring it to the surface again. A tube of mercury was arranged to mark the depth of descent.

It had been the design of the inventor to approach near to an enemy, then to submerge the boat and pass under the ship to be attacked, towing a floating torpedo to be exploded by means of electricity as soon as it touched the keel. Insufficient depth of water in the harbor prevented this manner of using the boat, however, and so she was rigged with a long spar at the bow, to which a torpedo was attached, to be fired by actual concussion with the object to be destroyed. This change necessarily made the boat more unwieldy, and probably had something to do with the tragic circumstances of her after-history.

The Navy Department offered to have one of its officers attached to the boat, but the request was refused on the grounds that an inexperienced hand would hinder, rather than help, the enterprise. After another spell of inactivity, the limit of Beauregard's forbearance was reached. Caution simply was no longer an acceptable option. Beauregard ordered the vessel seized and its civilian crew replaced with volunteers from the Confederate Navy.

Given command was Lieutenant John A. Payne, late of the *CSS Chicora*. Payne was as reckless as McClintock was cautious, but under the circumstances this was regarded a plus. The crew of the *Chicora* had distinguished themselves seven months earlier when their ironclad and its sister ram, the *Palmetto State*, daringly attacked the Union fleet outside Charleston in a thick morning fog. During the one-sided battle a Federal steamer surrendered and another was crippled, its ruptured boiler scalding to death twenty bluejackets. General Beauregard was ecstatic to the point of declaring the blockade lifted.

The *Chicora* seemed blessed. From the day it was commissioned in September 1862 until it was purposely blown up two and a half years later to prevent its capture, the ironclad was never damaged in an engagement and never suffered a single casualty. In fact, its only losses would be when several personnel volunteered for an even more hazardous duty—submarine service.

In addition to Payne, one other officer and four seamen—Michael Cane, Nicholas Davis, Frank Doyle, and John Kelly—transferred over from the *Chicora*. The officer was Payne's good friend, Lieutenant Charles Hasker. Hasker, an English immigrant, had gotten his baptism of fire as a boatswain on the *Virginia* during its historic duel with the *Monitor*. Like Payne, he had long demonstrated an interest in iron boats, both ironclads and submersibles.

Rounding out the nine-man crew were Absolum Williams, a volunteer from the *Palmetto State*; Charles L. Sprague, a torpedo expert and the only civilian on board; and Jeremiah Donivan, an eighteen-year-old former employee of the Park and Lyons shop in Mobile, where the submarine had been built. He was the only holdover from McClintock's original crew. McClintock and Watson hung around Charleston to act as advisors.

It was at this time that "Whitney's submarine boat," also variously referred to as the "Porpoise," the "Fish Boat," and the "cigar boat" by locals, appears to have been named the *H. L. Hunley*. (The name change was of no concern to investor and namesake Gus

Leaving Charleston. The unprecedented Union bombardment of August 1863 forced many citizens to flee the city for safer quarters in Columbia and elsewhere. Their leaving coincided with the arrival of Horace Hunley's "Fish" from Mobile.

Whitney, who before the year was out succumbed to pneumonia, the result of spending too many damp nights inside the vessel.) The "CSS" prefix, designating it as a Confederate States Ship, was attached then or soon afterwards.

Undoubtedly stung by his demotion, McClintock knew that operating the vessel was not as uncomplicated as it appeared. "The boat and machinery was so very simple," he stated years later, "that many persons at first inspection believed that they could work the boat without practice, or experience, and although I endeavored to prevent inexperienced persons from going underwater in the craft, I was not always successful in preventing them."

Payne, taking his cue from his superiors, rushed his raw crew through several training sessions. On August 29, 1863, just a day or two after taking command of the boat, Payne put the vessel through a series of practice dives in anticipation of making an attack that evening. That afternoon the submarine was moored at the docks near Fort Johnson, on the south end of the bay, when disaster struck.

According to Lieutenant Hasker, who was serving as first officer, Payne was climbing into the forward hatchway, preparing to shove off, when he became fouled by the hawser. In trying to clear himself, Payne "got his foot on the lever which controlled the fins.

Charleston Septbr 19th 1863.

General JT Beauregard.

Sir

I am a part owner of the torpedo boat the Hunley. I have been interested in building this description of boat since the beginning of the war, and furnished the means entirely of building the predecessor of this boat which was lost in an attempt to blow up a Federal vessel off fort Morgan Mobile Harbor. I feel therefore a deep interest in its success. I propose if you will place the boat in my hands to furnish a crew (in whole or in part) from Mobile who are well acquainted with the management, & make the attempt to destroy a vessel of the enemy as early as practicable

Very Respectfully,
Your Obt servt,
H.L. Hunley.

After an inexperienced crew caused the *Hunley* to sink during a training mission, part owner Horace L. Hunley wrote this letter to General Beauregard, requesting that he be put in command of the vessel.

He had just previously given the order to go ahead. The boat made a dive while the manholes were open and filled rapidly." The steamer *Etiwan*, sitting astern, suddenly cruised past, its ropes getting entangled with the *Hunley*. The submarine quickly filled with water and capsized.

While Payne escaped from the forward hatchway and Donivan and Sprague scrambled out of the aft hole, the other six men went down with the boat. One was Hasker, who years later described his remarkable escape.

"I had to get over the bar which connected the fins and through the manhole," he said. "This I did by forcing myself through the column of water which was rapidly filling the boat. The manhole plate came down on my back; but I worked my way out until my left leg was caught by the plate, pressing the calf of my leg in two. Held in this manner, I was carried to the bottom in forty-two feet of water.

Battery Wagner, an earthen redoubt on the north end of Morris Island, was one of several Confederate strongholds defending Charleston. Colonel Robert Gould Shaw, a Harvard graduate and the son of a wealthy Boston abolitionist, commanded the 54th Massachusetts Colored Regiment during the failed Federal attack on Battery Wagner in July 1863. The ferocious assault killed Shaw and hundreds of soldiers and inspired the 1989 movie, *Glory*. After enduring another seven weeks of siege, the fort's garrison were quietly evacuated across Charleston Harbor, ending what one observer called the "most fatal and fruitless campaign of the entire war."

"When the boat touched bottom I felt the [water] pressure relax. Stooping down I took hold of the manhole plate, drew out my wounded limb, and swam to the surface. . . . I was the only man that went to the bottom with the 'Fish Boat' and came up to tell the tale."

Not so lucky were Cane, Davis, Doyle, Kelly, and Williams. Cold water poured in and could not be stopped. Hysteria rose with the water inside the darkened chamber, until their shouts and flailing limbs were overcome by the unrelenting rush of seawater. "Poor fellows," said Theodore A. Honour, a soldier stationed at Fort Johnson, "they were five in one coffin."

Morale, already low among civilians and troops because of the loss of Fort Wagner on September 7 after two months of siege, plunged as fast and deep as the *Hunley* when news of this latest catastrophe spread through Charleston. Gus Smythe, stationed aboard the *Palmetto State*, mourned the loss of his friend, Williams. He spoke for many in a letter to his wife. "They were all volunteers for the expedition and fine men too, the best we had. It has cast quite a gloom over us. Strange, isn't it, that while we hear with indifference of men being killed all around us, the drowning of one should effect us so."

Two veteran civilian divers, Angus Smith and David Broadfoot, got the assignment to bring the *Hunley* back to the surface. Aside from the usual dangers associated with hard-hat diving, there were difficulties galore. The *Hunley* was stuck fast in the soft, muddy floor, forcing the divers to tunnel their way through the silt beneath the keel in order to wrap it in heavy hoist chains. Their labor took place a mere 200 yards from Fort Sumter, which was slowly being atomized by a continuous Union bombardment. For their work Angus and Broadfoot billed the government $300.

Following days of strenuous effort in the murky water, the *Hunley* was raised and its water-filled hull pumped dry. Inside was a frightful tableau. After ten days in the water, the bodies of the five drowned men were bloated, decomposed, malodorous, and as stiff as the iron walls that entombed them. Fish and crabs had nibbled at them. The rigor mortis forced the recovery team to saw off some limbs in order to fit the victims through the hatchways.

Hunley helped oversee the boat's salvage and retrofit, rounding up the scrub brushes, lime, and labor needed to thoroughly rid the

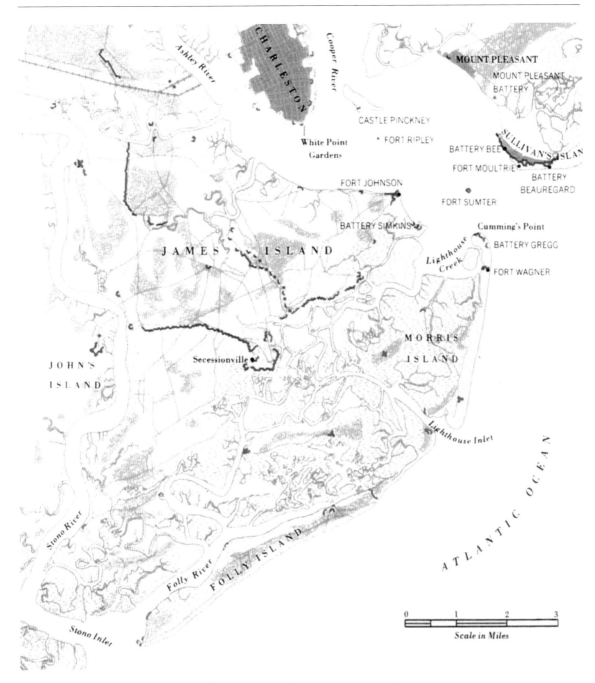

inside of the diving machine of any traces of its recent grisly history. On September 19, three weeks after the tragedy, he wrote a letter to Beauregard requesting that the salvaged vessel be placed
under his control and that he be allowed to furnish it with an experienced crew from Mobile. That crew, of course, was the very one
that had been dismissed in favor of its military replacement. If
granted his wish, Hunley promised to "make the attempt to destroy
a vessel of the enemy as early as practicable."

The general considered the offer. The Navy Department really had no idea of what to do with the vessel, especially in the light of the debacle that had occurred while under its control. A minor consideration may have been the $27,500 the cash-poor Confederate government owed the Singer Submarine Corps. That was the value of the *Hunley* as determined by a board of appraisers after the military seized the boat. Evidently it had yet to be paid.

(Although Hunley dealt with an intermediary, General Jordan, it's interesting to note the similarities in his and Beauregard's backgrounds. Both had been members of New Orleans's social elite before the war; Beauregard's family had made its fortune in sugar cane, a crop that had helped bring wealth to Hunley. They held similar views on the necessity of slavery, the inferiority of Negroes, and the joys to be found in mathematics, engineering, and amiable women. Moreover, between 1853 and 1860 Beauregard, then a captain in the army, spent the bulk of his time as the supervising engineer of the U. S. Customs House in New Orleans. The customhouse, which still stands at Decatur and Canal streets, was at the time the largest government structure ever built. Construction had originally begun in 1848, but within a few years the unfinished granite building was sinking into the moist soil. Beauregard expertly shored up the edifice, though by the outbreak of war the project had cost the government nearly $3 million and was still twenty years from being completed to its present four-story height. It's not difficult to imagine Hunley, who during this period was deputy collector of customs, sharing a reminiscence with the general about this boondoggle.)

Three days after Hunley's request, General Jordan instructed the arsenal commander to assist Captain Hunley and the mechanics assigned to him in any way possible. The inventor was back in charge of his own boat.

But not command. Although it's obvious that Hunley knew a great deal about submarines and had probably, on occasion, worked the controls of all three boats he was involved with, neither Beauregard nor the Navy Department were confident of his experience. Instead, Lieutenant George A. Dixon, who had successfully commanded the boat during its trials in Mobile, was dispatched to Charleston.

Most of the rest of the crew hailed from Mobile. In addition to Thomas Park, the son of one of the co-owners of the Park and Lyons shop, the other volunteers included Henry Beard, Robert

THE *CSS HUNLEY* AT CHARLESTON:
A Color Gallery

The *CSS H. L. Hunley* arrived in Charleston,
South Carolina, on August 15, 1863. Within
six months the ill-fated submarine would
change the course of naval history.

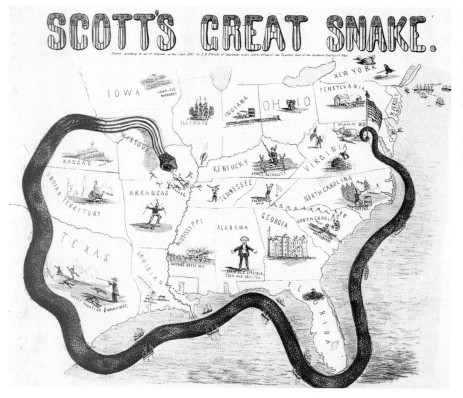

An Ohio newspaper had fun with Union General Winfield Scott's plan to bring the Confederacy to its knees through an ambitious economic blockade, but ultimately "Scott's Great Snake" worked. The *Hunley* was moved from Mobile to Charleston in the summer of 1863 for the purpose of attacking Federal ironclads.

General Pierre Gustave Toutant Beauregard, the Confederate military commander of Charleston, looks appropriately heroic in this full-length painting, one of several tributes to be found today around the city. It was upon Beauregard's request that the *Hunley* was shipped to Charleston, though the general was never fully convinced of its effectiveness.

This fanciful sketch of the *Hunley* was made by a Union artist with no first-hand knowledge of the Rebel innovation. Among the inaccuracies were populating the submersible with thirteen crew members and neglecting to link the drive shaft to the propeller.

The *Hunley*, docked at Charleston, was painted by Conrad Wise Chapman in December 1863, just weeks after a training accident had claimed the lives of its namesake and seven other men.

The Confederate torpedo boat *Little David* near the Charleston docks in 1863. The steam-powered vessel was fifty feet long, had a crew of four, and was armed with a 100-pound torpedo attached to a fourteen-foot spar. The David-class boats sat low in the water, but they were not true submersibles. The *Little David*'s daring attack on the *New Ironsides* on October 5, 1863, renewed hopes that submarines could break the Union blockade.

Confederate keg mines like this one were no barrel of laughs for the Federal fleet at Charleston. The underwater explosive consisted of wooden cones attached to both ends of a beer keg, which was filled with gunpowder and outfitted with sensitive fuses. The cones provided stability while an anchor held the crude mine a few inches beneath the water's surface. A moderate blow from an unsuspecting vessel was enough to set off an explosion.

The bow of the *Hunley*, like those of the David-class torpedo boats, was fitted with a "deadly stinger"—a spar torpedo designed to deliver an explosive from a safe distance. A postwar article described how the system worked: "Its front was terminated by a sharp and barbed lance-head so that when the boat was driven end on against a ship's sides, the lance head would be forced deep into the timbers below the water line, and would fasten the torpedo firmly against the ship. Then the torpedo boat would back off and explode it by a lanyard."

The *Hunley* makes a surface run on a clear night in this computer-generated illustration by Daniel Dowdey.

An explosion rips apart the hull of the *USS Housatonic* on the evening of February 17, 1864, the result of the *Hunley* detonating a torpedo against the victim's stern. Within minutes the crippled *Housatonic* will sink and the *Hunley* will vanish, a mutually destructive encounter that marks the first successful submarine attack in history.

Brookbank, John Marshall, Charles McHugh, and Joseph Patterson. Evidently all were fellow shop employees. In fact, it's possible that some or all had belonged to McClintock's original crew, the one that was relieved by Beauregard; however, because the identities of the first crew has never been established, this is strictly conjecture. They were joined by torpedo expert Charles Sprague, who had survived the sinking of August 29.

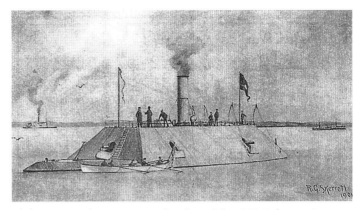

The CSS *Palmetto State*. The *Hunley* practiced mock attacks on the iron-clad.

By the first week of October, the crew had been assembled and was honing its skills in the Cooper River. With Dixon in the forward hatch, operating the diving planes, and Park acting as first officer, taking care of the ballast tank pumps and sea valves, the *Hunley* repeatedly practiced dives under the *CSS Indian Chief*. As in past drills, the goal was to draw the dummy torpedo it was dragging against the target vessel's hull, a maneuver that the crew quickly became adept at. In fewer than two weeks, the *Hunley* seemed to be nearly ready. A new compass had been installed and 200 feet of thickly braided rope, needed to tow the torpedo, had also arrived.

On the gray, drizzly morning of October 15, 1863, the *Hunley* embarked on yet another practice run. At the helm this time was Captain Hunley, who was filling in for Dixon, away from Charleston on some unnamed business.

The boat left the dock at 9:25 A.M. Within ten minutes it was within a couple hundred feet of the *Indian Chief*. Hunley took one final navigational finding, the hatches were closed, the diving planes depressed, and the vessel slowly dipped beneath the waves.

Then suddenly, inexplicably, something went wrong.

After a few minutes crew members of the *Indian Chief* became anxious. After so many mock attacks, they had grown accustomed to the routine. They had expected to see the *Hunley* reappear on its port side. They scanned the surface for signs of the submersible. The minutes dragged. A few bubbles appeared, but that was it. By noon, more than two hours after the *Hunley* submerged, the sad truth had settled in. The following day the local paper briefly reported on a "Melancholy Occurrence." Readers learned that there had been an accident involving a "small boat in Cooper River, containing eight persons, all of whom were drowned."

Once again the salvage services of divers Angus Smith and David Broadfoot were enlisted. They donned their copper helmets and discovered the wreck on October 18 in fifty-four feet of water, its bow jammed into the muddy sea bottom at an angle. Just as the raising tackle and hoist boats were ready, a storm blew in from the northeast, whipping up waves and delaying recovery for an entire week.

Finally, with good weather and a calm tide, Smith and Broadfoot descended into the frigid gloom and resumed their grim task. On November 6, as the final preparations were being made to raise the vessel, General Beauregard instructed "the remains of Captain Hunley buried with the military honors due to an officer of his rank."

The following evening, three and a half weeks after it had plowed into the muddy floor of Charleston Harbor, the *Hunley* was finally hauled to the surface. As word was delivered to Beauregard and the submarine's investors, excited citizens hurried down to the wharf at the foot of Calhoun Street. One, a sixteen-year-old boy named R. M. Haddon, later recalled that, even before the hatch bolts were broken open, several men volunteered on the spot to take the place of the dead crew inside.

Awaiting all on the dock that night was a spectacle that Beauregard later recorded as "indescribably ghastly." The hatch was pried open, releasing a rush of fetid gas and revealing eight macabre mannequins "contorted into all kinds of horrible attitudes, some clutching candles, evidently endeavoring to force open the man-holes; others lying in the bottom, tightly grappled together, and the blackened faces of all presented the expression of their despair and agony." No reports document the actual removal of the victims, but it seems likely that, once again, the stiff, swollen bodies had to be at least partially dismembered to get them through the narrow hatchways.

Hunley was the first to be removed. He was placed inside a "fine lined coffin" arranged by Gardner Smith, a close friend that Hunley had summoned from Mobile. Smith arrived in Charleston on October 18,

The November 9, 1863, edition of the *Daily Mercury* recorded the fate of Horace Hunley and his crew, all asphyxiated during a training mishap three and a half weeks earlier.

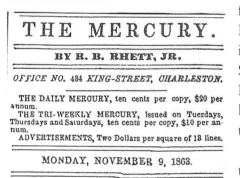

THE MERCURY.

BY R. B. RHETT, JR.

OFFICE NO. 484 KING-STREET, CHARLESTON.

THE DAILY MERCURY, ten cents per copy, $20 per annum.
THE TRI-WEEKLY MERCURY, issued on Tuesdays, Thursdays and Saturdays, ten cents per copy, $10 per annum.
ADVERTISEMENTS, Two Dollars per square of 18 lines.

MONDAY, NOVEMBER 9, 1863.

LAST HONORS TO A DEVOTED PATRIOT.—The remains of Captain HORACE L. HUNLEY were yesterday interred in Magnolia Cemetery. His body was followed to the grave by a military escort, and a large number of citizens.

The deceased was a native of Tennessee, but for many years past has been a resident of New Orleans.

Possessed of an ample fortune, in the prime of manhood—for he was only thirty-six at the time of his death—with everything before him to make life attractive, he came to Charleston, and voluntarily joined in a patriotic enterprise which promised success, but which was attended with great peril. Though feeling, as appears from the last letter which he wrote to his friends, a presentiment that he would perish in the adventure, he gave his whole heart, undeterred by the foreboding, to the undertaking, declaring that he would gladly sacrifice his life in the cause. That presentiment has been mournfully fulfilled. Yet who shall call that fate a sad one, which associates the name of its victim with those of his country's most unselfish martyrs?

only to discover to his shock that the *Hunley* had been lost three days earlier. The heavy-hearted Smith could do nothing beyond telegraphing the awful news to Hunley's friends and relatives and seeing to it that the captain and his crew received a proper send-off.

Meanwhile, he and others pondered what had gone wrong. It wasn't until thirty-eight years later that William Alexander, the most prolific postwar chronicler of the vessel's history, detailed the probable cause of the disaster.

"The position in which the boat was found on the bottom of the river, the condition of the apparatus discovered after it was raised and pumped out, and the position of the bodies in the boat, furnished a full explanation for her loss," he wrote in the *New Orleans Picayune* of June 29, 1902:

> Captain Hunley's body was forward, with his head in the forward hatchway, his right hand on top of his head (he had been trying, it would seem, to raise the hatch cover). In his left hand was a candle that had never been lighted. The sea-cock on the forward end, or *Hunley*'s ballast tank, was wide open, the cock-wrench not on the plug, but lying on the bottom of the boat. Mr. Park's body was found with his head in the after hatchway, his right hand above his head. He also had been trying to raise the hatch cover, but the pressure was too great. The sea-cock to his tank was properly closed, and the tank was nearly empty. The other bodies were floating in the water. Hunley and Parks were undoubtedly asphyxiated, the others drowned. The bolts that had held the iron keel ballast had been partly turned, but not sufficient to release it.
>
> In the light of these conditions, we can easily depict before our minds, and almost readily explain, what took place in the boat during the moments immediately following its submergence.
>
> Captain Hunley's practice with the boat had made him quite familiar and expert in handling her, and this familiarity produced at this time forgetfulness. It was found in practice to be easier on the crew to come to the surface by giving the pumps a few strokes and ejecting some of the water ballast, than by the momentum of the boat operating on the elevated fins. At this time the boat was under way, lighted through the dead-lights in the hatchways. He partly turned the fins to go down, but thought, no doubt, that he needed more ballast and opened his sea cock. Immediately the boat was in total darkness.
>
> He then undertook to light the candle. While trying to do

this the tank quietly flooded, and under great pressure the boat sank very fast and soon overflowed, and the first intimation they would have of anything being wrong was the water rising fast, but noiselessly, about their feet in the bottom of the boat. They tried to release the iron keel ballast, but did not turn the keys quite far enough, therefore failed. The water soon forced the air to the top of the boat and into the hatchways, where captains Hunley and Park were found. Park had pumped his ballast tank dry, and no doubt Captain Hunley had exhausted himself on his pump, but he had forgotten that he had not closed his sea cock.

Once again human error, not mechanical failure, had cost the submarine a crew. This time Captain Hunley had inadvertently left the valve to the front ballast tank open, causing it to overflow and the sub to plunge nine fathoms at an angle into the sea floor. All Hunley needed to do was close the valve at any time and the water that had spilled over from the ballast tank and into the cabin could have been pumped out. Instead, the valve handle was lost somewhere in the bilges, its discovery hampered by the darkness, jumbled bodies, rising water, and general state of confusion. The *Hunley* was equipped with a 250-pound keel weight, an emergency device whose release theoretically should have floated the boat free. However, the bolts holding it in place had only been loosened, not completely undone, indicating either a panicky attempt or that the keel weight was jammed in place by the angle of the hull. The terrified crew had undoubtedly worked the pumps like madmen, but it was impossible to empty a tank that remained open to the sea.

November 8 was a Sunday. That afternoon, the Reverend W. B. Yates performed a "solemn and impressive" Episcopalian funeral service for Hunley that included a military escort of two companies and a band. The procession slowly wound its way through Charleston's streets to Magnolia Cemetery, a burial ground established in 1850 on the banks of the Cooper River.

The next day's *Mercury* reported on the "Last Honors to a Devoted Patriot."

> The remains of Captain Horace L. Hunley were yesterday interred in Magnolia Cemetery. His body was followed to the grave by a military escort, and a large number of citizens.
>
> The deceased was a native of Tennessee, but for many years past has been a resident of New Orleans.
>
> Possessed of an ample fortune, in the prime of manhood—

for he was only thirty-six at the time of his death—with everything before him to make life attractive, he came to Charleston, and voluntarily joined in a patriotic enterprise which promised success, but which was attended with great peril. Though feeling, as appears from the last letter which he wrote to his friends, a presentiment that he would perish in the adventure, he gave his whole heart, undeterred by the foreboding, to the undertaking, declaring that he would gladly sacrifice his life in the cause. That presentiment has been mournfully fulfilled. Yet who shall call that fate a sad one, which associates the name of its victim with those of his country's most unselfish martyrs?

On November 9 the rest of the crew—Park, Beard, Brookbank, Marshall, McHugh, Patterson, and Sprague—were buried in a lot adjoining Hunley's. Gardner Smith selected a small tombstone whose inscription described their captain as "A native of Tennessee, but for many years a citizen of New Orleans, who lost his life in the service of his country." Many years later the Charleston County Centennial Commission erected a marker on the plot known today as "Hunley Circle."

In conversations and in letters, most people were properly reverential when addressing the tragedy and its victims. "At the grave I could not refrain from tears as the casket of the spirit of a noble and generous man was being lowered, 'earth to earth,' to its final resting place," Smith wrote Hunley's younger sister, Louisa, in New Orleans. "I lost in him my best friend. . . . He was so gentlemanly and so kind."

Among sailors and garrison troops, however, this latest undersea disaster was spoken of in less refined terms. Those aware of the *Hunley*'s reputation had often referred to it as "the peripatetic coffin." Now the vessel to which yet another crew had plunged to their unspeakable deaths had acquired a new name. It was called "the murdering machine."

Lieutenant George Dixon, the last commander of the *Hunley*.

Chapter Four

ATTACK
ON THE
HOUSATONIC

On October 16, 1863, the day after the *Hunley* was reported missing, Lieutenant George Dixon was given orders to return to Mobile. Accompanying him was a Confederate secret agent named Henry Dillingham, an accomplished saboteur of Union property. Given the character of Dillingham's work, it's not too surprising that the exact nature of his involvement with the submarine has never been established. It probably involved, in part, his expertise with explosive devices. Beyond that, his role remains a mystery.

Within a couple of days Dixon and Dillingham were inside the Park and Lyons machine shop, somberly informing an anxious group of employees that some of their friends, including the business owner's son, Tom Park, had disappeared and were presumed drowned. After that Dixon pleaded his case to the military authorities for permission to assume command of the vessel, once it was raised from the floor of Charleston harbor and refitted.

"I can have nothing more to do with that submarine boat," General Beauregard responded via telegraph. "It's more dangerous to those who use it than the enemy." But Dixon would eventually get his way.

(No 40.)

SPECIAL REQUISITION.

For　Sub marine Torpedo Boat H L Hunley

Nov 17ᵗ　5 Scrubbing Brushes

1 Bble of Lime

1 Box of Soap　2½ pounds

" 23ᵈ　2 pound of Cotton Rope

Dec 7ᵗ　15　"　"　"

1　"　of Cotton　"

One Compass for Boat

Two Paint Brushes

18 feet of 2½ Rope 5 lb

One Bucket

One Brass Sheave

I certify that the above Requisition is correct; and that the articles specified are absolutely requisite for the public ser-

vice rendered so by the following circumstances:　Lt Geo E. Dixon

Appd By Command Genl Beauregard

Maunpat

Quartermaster, C. S. Army, will issue the articles specified in the above requisition.

Lt Geo E. Dixon　Commanding.

Received at Charleston　the 15th of November 186 3 of

Maj. M. A. Pringle Quartermaster, C. S Army. the nine articles —

in full of the above requisition

(SIGNED DUPLICATES.)

Lt Geo E. Dixon

In the wake of the accident that claimed Horace Hunley and his crew, Lieutenant Dixon made out this requisition for cleaning brushes, lime, and other supplies to clean and refit the *Hunley*.

In addition to persistence, Dixon also had courage and self-confidence in abundance. "I never knew a better man," his commander, Captain John Cothran, told the *Montgomery Advisor* in a 1900 interview, "and there never was a braver man in any service of any army."

Dixon, who was in his middle twenties, cut a handsome figure. He had lanky blond hair, a fair complexion, and stood a shade under six feet tall. Dixon had a sweetheart living in Mobile. Queenie Bennett was the cute, feisty daughter of George Bennett, a steamboat captain on whose vessel Dixon had worked as an engineer before the war.

After the beginning of hostilities Dixon enlisted as a private in Company A of the 21st Alabama Infantry. When the regiment marched off to war, Queenie was one of the many pretty girls of Mobile who flocked to the train station to bid a tearful adieu. Before Dixon departed, Queenie pressed a twenty-dollar gold piece into his hand.

Dixon fought at the Battle of Shiloh the following spring, a two-day bloodbath that produced 23,500 casualties on both sides. Dixon was one of them. In the early morning hours of Sunday, April 6, 1862, he was struck in the left thigh by a Yankee bullet. Remarkably, it struck the coin in his pocket. Although the minié ball bent the coin and drove it into his flesh, its otherwise deadly impact had been absorbed. For the rest of his days, Dixon would carry the bell-shaped keepsake as a good luck charm.

By the second week of November, 1863, Dixon was back in Charleston. With him were Dillingham, Lieutenant William Alexander (also on detached duty from the 21st Alabama), and an unidentified associate.

Dixon renewed his pleas with headquarters to be put in charge of the *Hunley*. The funerals of Captain Hunley and his crew, held just days before, were fresh in the mind of General Beauregard. But after considerable discussion with his chief of staff, General Jordan, he finally relented. Assuming that his decision received the blessings of the Navy Department (which it soon did), the *Hunley* would be given one last chance to prove its worth.

Dixon, ecstatic, immediately dashed off a letter to Jordan.

"Before I can proceed with my work of cleaning the Sub-Marine boat," he wrote on November 14, "I shall have to request of you an order on the Quartermaster or Engineer Department for ten Negroes, also an order on the Commissary Department for soap, brushes, and lime, and an order on the Arsenal to have some work done at that place. In order to make all possible haste with this work, I would be pleased to have those orders granted at your earliest convenience."

The next day Dixon requisitioned five scrubbing brushes, a barrel of lime, a large box of soap, and a bucket (all for cleaning the fetid interior), as well as several lengths of rope, a new compass, and a brass pulley sheave.

The *Hunley* was cradled on a dock at Mount Pleasant, a fortified harbor town located northwest of Sullivan's Island. There it underwent a thorough cleaning, painting, and refitting. By the end of November the boat's overhaul was nearing completion and it was ready to be outfitted with a new crew. This last part wasn't easy—not for a lack of volunteers, but because of Beauregard's continuing reluctance to put more seamen at risk operating what had proven to be nothing but an unlucky, ineffective craft.

"We soon had the boat refitted and in good shape, reported to General Jordan that she was ready for service, and asked for a crew," recalled Lieutenant Alexander, who served as Dixon's first officer. "After many refusals and much discussion, General Beauregard finally assented to our going aboard the Confederate receiving ship *Indian Chief* and calling for volunteers. He strictly enjoined upon us to give a full and clear explanation of the desperately hazardous nature of the service required."

Dixon, of course, was no stranger to the crew of the *Indian Chief*. He had commanded the *Hunley* on most of its mock attacks on the *Indian Chief*, his familiar figure rising out of the forward hatchway, blond hair whipping in the wind, as the sub bore down on the target ship. Some of the barefoot sailors carefully listening to his and Alexander's pitch on the quarterdeck of the *Indian Chief* undoubtedly had reservations, though they kept their doubts to themselves. All retained the awful memory of October 15, when an earlier crew of eager volunteers had gone to their deaths. Some might have contributed to the fund being raised around Charleston to benefit the widows and orphans of the sailors who had perished with Captain Hunley. Nonetheless, the two young lieutenants encountered no difficulty in getting volunteers to man the *Hunley*.

Five sailors were selected: Arnold Becker, F. Collins, Ridgeway, C. Simkins, and James A. Wicks. Although the first names of some

of these sailors have unfortunately been lost to history, in the light of their intimate knowledge of the *Hunley*'s past each was an unquestionably brave man. Wicks, for example, had everything to live for: his wife, Catherine, and their four daughters, the oldest of whom, Eliza, was just ten years old. "I don't believe a man considered the danger which awaited him," claimed Alexander. "The honor of being first to engage the enemy in this novel way overshadowed all else."

Filling out the nine-man crew was the group from Mobile: Dixon, Alexander, Dillingham, and their anonymous companion. This completed a radical makeover in the composition of the group involved with the *Hunley* during its short but eventful life. Since the submarine first came to Charleston four months earlier, Captain Hunley and a dozen crew members had died; one of the survivors of its two accidents, Lieutenant Charles Hasker, had been captured on Morris Island; and two of its designers, Baxter Watson and James McClintock (who'd also served as skipper), were now assisting its principal investor, E. C. Singer, in mining Mobile harbor.

The new crew took up quarters at the Old Shell Hall on Ferry Street in Mount Pleasant, a combination arsenal-barracks. Although the *Hunley* was still cradled on the wharf, the newcomers were given a thorough indoctrination in the boat's operating and safety features, a course of instruction that probably took several days. Soon

As the U. S. Navy's most formidable ironclad, the *USS New Ironsides* inspired fear and hatred among the enemy. On the night of October 5, 1863, in an attempt to break the blockade of Charleston harbor, the *CSS David* exploded a spar torpedo against an unarmored portion of its 230-foot-long hull. An ensign wrote his mother: "it was a failure & most of the rebels were taken prisoners, the rest were drowned; the Ironside was not hurt, & only one man killed, but it rather scared them."

the boat was ready for actual practice dives in the waters around the harbor, its initially uneasy crew growing more comfortable inside their claustrophobic surroundings with every turn of the crankshaft. By early December Dixon felt confident enough to inform headquarters that the *Hunley* was combat ready.

On December 14, Beauregard issued the following special order:

> First Lieut. George E. Dixon, Twenty-first Regiment Alabama Volunteers, will take command and direction of the Submarine Torpedo-Boat "H. L. Hunley," and proceed to-night to the mouth of the harbor, or as far as capacity of the vessel will allow, and will sink and destroy any vessel of the enemy with which he can come in conflict.

Beginning that evening, Dixon maneuvered the *Hunley* past the crumbled walls of still defiant Fort Sumter, out of the harbor and into the open sea. These first sorties were unnerving. Tugs and picket boats protected the Union ironclads moored in the channel and calcium lights illuminated the dark waters. There also was the danger of the *Hunley* running aground on shoals and hidden sandbars. Meanwhile, the stronger currents played havoc with navigation and the torpedo it was towing. The mine drifted dangerously all over the place, remembered Alexander. "The torpedo was a copper cylinder holding a charge of ninety pounds of explosive, with percussion and primer mechanism, set off by triggers. It was originally intended to float the torpedo on the surface of the water, towed by the boat, which was to dive under the vessel to be attacked. In experiments made with some old flat boats in smooth water, this plan operated successfully, but in a seaway the torpedo was continually coming too near our craft."

Also of concern were the several miles the crew had to crank just to reach the harbor mouth, the jumping-off point for a foray against the ironclads. The men found themselves exhausted just as the most taxing part of the mission was beginning. To rectify the situation, Dixon requested a steam vessel to tow the *Hunley* into position. The legendary *CSS Little David* was assigned the task.

The steam-powered torpedo boat was fifty feet long, had a crew of four, and during combat missions was armed with a 100-pound torpedo attached to a fourteen-foot spar. This spar torpedo—aptly characterized as a "deadly stinger"—was designed to deliver an

A David-class torpedo boat lies beached after the capture of Charleston. This is possibly the original *David*, built in Charleston in 1863, which inspired the generic name used by the Federals for all Confederate torpedo boats.

explosive from a safe distance. A postwar article described how the system worked: "Its front was terminated by a sharp and barbed lance-head so that when the boat was driven end on against a ship's sides, the lance head would be forced deep into the timbers below the water line, and would fasten the torpedo firmly against the ship. Then the torpedo boat would back off and explode it by a lanyard."

The *Little David* actually was just one of an estimated twelve to fourteen torpedo boats built by the Confederacy; the Union used the generic term "David" for each of them. The David-class boats were cigar-shaped, sat low in the water, and ran with their decks awash, but were not true submersibles. Some were steam operated, others were propelled by hand cranking.

The *Little David* had participated in at least three attempts to break the blockade since being launched by builder David Ebaugh (hence the vessel's name) in 1863. The most daring attack was on the *USS New Ironsides*. The Union warship seemed impregnable. Officially classified as a steam frigate, nearly three-quarters of its 230-foot hull were covered with iron plates, four and a half inches thick. Unlike the turreted, double-gun ironclads, the *New Ironsides*'s firepower was massive and distributed in traditional broadside fashion. Its main battery featured sixteen eleven-inch Dahlgren guns. During an attack on Confederate defenses in early 1863, the armored ship was hit fifty times without effect. It was the most feared vessel in Admiral John Dahlgren's South Atlantic Blockading Squadron, protecting blockaders, shelling fortifications, and intercepting blockade runners. As such, the *New Ironsides* became the number-one target on Confederate Charleston's hit list, as evidenced by John Fraser & Company's open offer of $100,000 to anybody who could sink it.

Under the command of Lieutenant William T. Glassell, the *Little David* had launched its surprise attack on the armored flagship on the evening of October 5, 1863, driving a spar torpedo into an unprotected part of the starboard quarter. The ensuing explosion poured water into the torpedo boat's smokestack, dousing its boiler. With his boat dead in the water, Glassell ordered it abandoned. Glassell and one crew member were captured, but acting engineer J. H. Tomb braved a hail of enemy gunfire to swim back to the *Little David*, where he and the pilot rebuilt the fires, got steam up, and escaped. The damage to the *New Ironsides* was not serious, and only one Union officer was killed, but news of the daring attack and improbable escape excited Charleston and resulted in Tomb's taking over command of the *Little David*. It also revived expectations that a submarine, with its ability to act with even greater stealth than the low-slung torpedo boat, could break the Union blockade. But ten days later the *Hunley* went down in Charleston harbor, claiming the lives of Captain Hunley and a second crew and extinguishing hopes. Now Tomb was playing a role in bringing those hopes back to life.

Because of the demonstrated success of the spar torpedo in the *New Ironsides* action, Tomb naturally frowned on the *Hunley*'s method of delivering its payload. A towed torpedo was less reliable and more dangerous to its crew than a "deadly stinger." Should the sub "attempt to use a torpedo as Lieutenant Dixon intended," Tomb wrote in a report to his superiors, "by submerging the boat and striking from below, the level of the torpedo would be above his own boat, and as she had little buoyancy and no power, the chances were the suction caused by the water passing into the sinking ship would prevent her from rising to the surface."

Tomb's critical view was reinforced by a nearly disastrous incident. One evening in January 1864, he was towing the *Hunley* out of the harbor when the submarine's drifting torpedo line became tied up in the torpedo boat's rudder assembly. All that was needed for a major catastrophe was for the highly sensitive mine, now bobbing alongside the vessels, to bang into either hull. Although it was a winter night, both crews sweated through their clothes waiting for one unidentified brave soul to jump into the water and disentangle the fouled line. It was the last time the *Little David* ever towed the *Hunley*. From then on another vessel, unnamed, performed the task.

The *Hunley* became a familiar sight around Charleston over the winter of 1863–64. Rumors of its existence were verified to the Federal fleet by a Confederate deserter, who provided his interrogators with a fairly accurate account of its troubled history and even made a model of it. Thanks to the capture of Lieutenant Glassell the previous October, Admiral Dahlgren already knew many of the mechanical particulars of the *Little David* and similar semisubmersibles. Concerned with the danger both kinds of vessels posed to his fleet, he issued the following order on January 7, 1864:

This copper-jacketed spar torpedo was designed to be attached to the end of a long pole projecting from the bow of an attacking David-class torpedo boat or submarine.

> I have reliable information that the Rebels have two torpedo boats ready for service, which may be expected on the first night when the weather is suitable for their movement. One of these is the *David* which attacked the *Ironsides* in October, the other is similar to it.
>
> There is also one of another kind, which is nearly submerged, and can be entirely so; it is intended to go under the bottoms of vessels and there operate. This is believed by my information to be sure of well working, though from bad management it has hereto met with accidents, and was lying off Mount Pleasant two nights since. There being every reason to expect a visit from some or all of these torpedoes, the greatest vigilance will be needed to guard against them. The ironclads must have their fenders rigged out, and their own boats in motion about them. A netting must also be dropped overboard from the ends of the fenders, kept down with shot, and extended along the whole length of the sides; howitzers loaded with canister on the decks and a calcium for each monitor.
>
> The tugs and picket boats must be incessantly upon the lookout, whether the weather is clear or rainy. I observe the ironclads are not anchored so as to be entirely clear of each other's fire if opened suddenly in the dark. This must be corrected, and Captain Rowan will assign the monitors suitable positions for this purpose, particularly with reference to his own vessel.
>
> It is also advisable not to anchor in the deepest part of the channel; for by not leaving much space between the bottom of the vessel and the bottom of the channel, it will be impossible for the diving torpedo to operate except on the sides, and there will be less difficulty in raising a vessel if sunk.

Tension and fear can be read on the faces of the nine crew members of the *Hunley* as the submariners test the vessel's—and their own—underwater endurance. Despite diminished oxygen and the claustrophobic conditions, the *Hunley* could stay submerged for as long as two and a half hours.

The *Hunley* makes a sur-
face run by moonlight.

The Federal fleet pounds
away at Fort Moultrie.

Dahlgren's directive changed the game for Dixon's intrepid group. The ironclads lying near the harbor's entrance had been their original objective, but the increased security precautions forced Dixon and Alexander to turn their sights elsewhere. Their eyes settled on the main squadron of wooden warships, anchored far off shore. The nearest was the *USS Wabash*, a wooden-hulled steam frigate lying twelve miles out. Lesser men might have given up. Instead, the *Hunley*'s base was relocated to Battery Marshall, an earthen fortification that guarded the eastern end of Sullivan's Island. From there the *Hunley* would be in a better position to attack its intended victim.

At this time the *Hunley* was outfitted with a spar torpedo. This weapon was useless against the armor plating of the Union monitors. But with the ironclads no longer the target, and the *Hunley* now planning to head out into heavier seas, the old practice of towing a contact mine was deemed riskier and less effective than employing a spar torpedo.

Through the early part of 1864, the crew of the *Hunley* fell into a daily routine, leaving their base at Mount Pleasant every afternoon about one o'clock and walking the beach the seven miles to Battery Marshall. Following the beach path "exposed us to fire," said Alexander, "but it was the best walking."

They would take the *Hunley* out into the back bay for two or three hours of practice, trying to familiarize themselves with the new spar torpedo.

"Dixon and myself would then stretch out on the beach with the compass between us," said Alexander, "and get the bearings of the nearest vessel as she took her position for the night; ship up the torpedo on the boom, and, when dark, go out, steering for the vessel, proceed until the condition of the men, sea, tide, wind, moon, and daylight compelled our return to the dock; unship the torpedo, put it under guard at Battery Marshall, walk back to our quarters at Mount Pleasant, and cook breakfast."

The men would catch whatever sleep they could during the day before returning to their base of operations for, conditions permitting, another grueling nocturnal foray. This being January, the headwinds were wicked, kicking up the waves and slowing their progress considerably.

"In comparatively smooth water and light current the *Hunley* could make four miles an hour," remembered Alexander, "but in rough water the speed was much slower. It was winter, therefore necessary that we go out with the ebb and come in with the flood tide, a fair wind, and dark moon. This latter was essential to our success, as our experience had fully demonstrated the necessity of occasionally coming to the surface, slightly lifting the after hatch-cover, and letting in a little air. On several occasions we came to the

An interior view of Fort Moultrie.

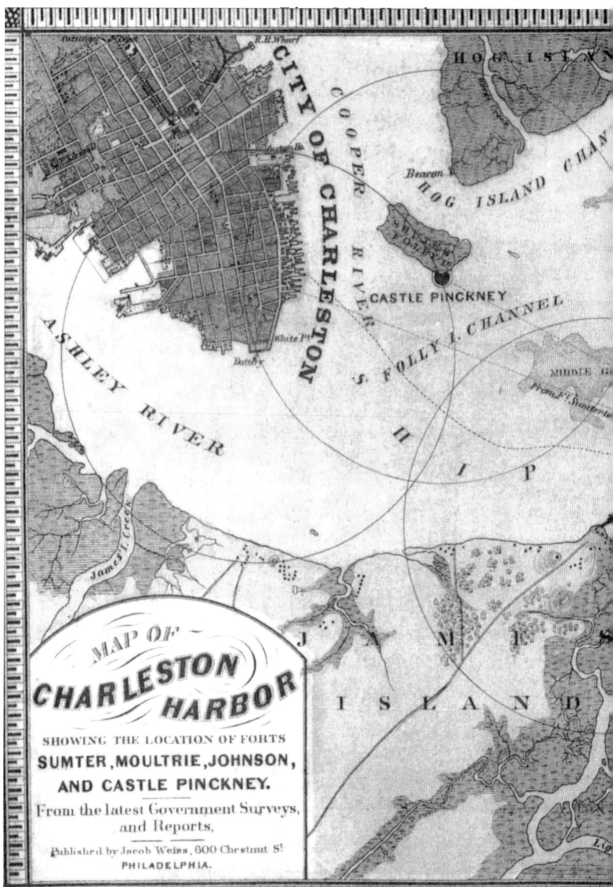

MAP OF
CHARLESTON HARBOR

SHOWING THE LOCATION OF FORTS
SUMTER, MOULTRIE, JOHNSON,
AND CASTLE PINCKNEY.

From the latest Government Surveys,
and Reports,

Published by Jacob Weiss, 600 Chestnut St.
PHILADELPHIA.

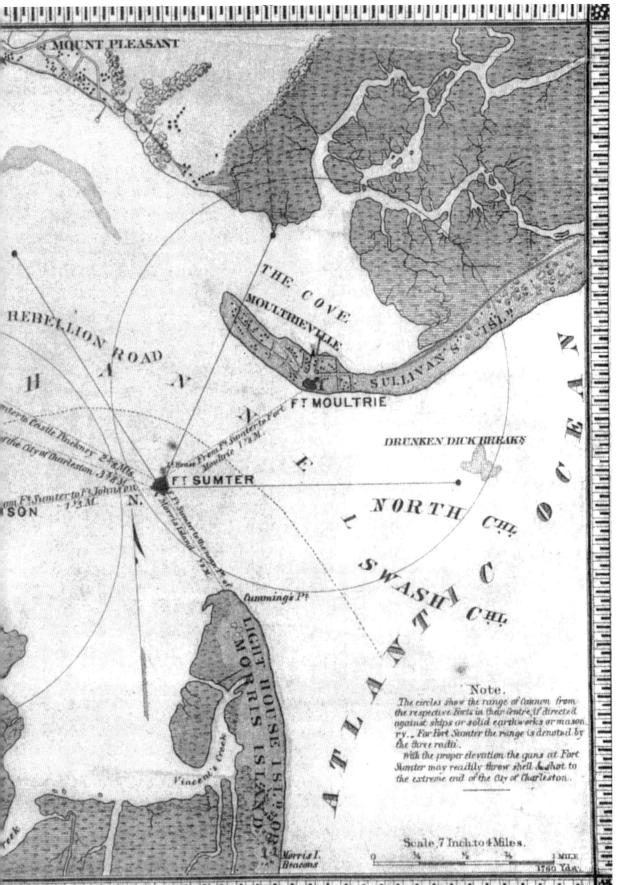

MOUNT PLEASANT

THE COVE

MOULTRIEVILLE

SULLIVAN'S ISL.^D

FT. MOULTRIE

REBELLION ROAD

H A N N E L

...ter to Castle Pinckney 2¾ Mls.
...the City of Charleston 3¾ M.

Light house from Ft Sumter to Fort
Moultrie 1⅓ M.

... Ft Sumter to Ft Johns 1½.
SON   1½ M.

N.

Ft Sumter to the Light ... Ft
Morris Island 1½ M.

FT SUMTER

DRUNKEN DICK BREAKS

NORTH   CH¹.

E   L   SWASH

Cumming's Pt

A   T   L   A   N   T   C

O C E A N

LIGHT HOUSE ISL.^D OR

MORRIS ISLAND

Vincent's Creek

Creek

Morris I.
Beacons

Note.

The circles show the range of Cannon from
the respective Forts in their Centre, if directed
against ships or solid earthworks or masonry., For Fort Sumter the range is denoted by
the three radii.

With the proper elevation the guns at Fort
Sumter may readily throw shell & shot to
the extreme end of the City of Charleston.

Scale 7 Inch to 4 Miles.

0   ¼   ½   ¾   1 MILE

1760 Yds.

Rear Admiral John A. Dahlgren, who established and directed the U. S. Navy's ordnance department before the war, assumed command of the South Atlantic Blockading Squadron in July 1863. Among his contributions to naval ordnance were bronze boat howitzers and rifles, iron rifles, and iron smoothbore shellguns, all of which were used to great effect during the war.

surface for air, opened the cover, and heard the men in the Federal picket boats talking and singing."

Alexander stated that the *Hunley* went out on the average of four nights a week during this period. Bad weather and exhaustion usually forced the submarine to turn around after going six or seven miles. "This we always found a task," Alexander said, "and many times it taxed our utmost exertions to keep from drifting out to sea, daylight often breaking while we were yet in range."

Building stamina was of paramount importance. Everything was geared towards conditioning the men to make their way ten or more miles out to sea, mounting a successful attack, and returning safely. Part of this conditioning involved a test to see how long the crew could remain submerged without replenishing the boat's supply of oxygen. Alexander later wrote a detailed account of the experiment:

It was agreed by all hands to sink and let the boat rest on the bottom in the back bay off Battery Marshall, each man to make equal physical exertion in turning the propeller. It was also agreed that if anyone in the crew felt he must come to the surface for air and he gave the word "Up," we would at once bring the boat to the surface.

It was usual when practicing near the bay that the banks would be lined with soldiers. One evening after alternately diving and rising many times, Dixon and myself and several of the crew compared watches, noted the time and sank for the test. In twenty-five minutes after I had closed the after manhead and excluded the outer air, the candle would not burn. Dixon forward and myself aft turned on the propeller tanks as hard as we could. In comparing our individual experiences afterwards, the experience of one was found to be the experience of all. Each man had determined that he would not be the first man to say

"Up." Not a word was said except an occasional "How is it?" between Dixon and myself until the "Up!" came from all nine. We started the pumps. Dixon's worked all right but mine was not throwing [water]. From experience I guessed the cause of the failure, took off the cap of the pump, looked at the valve and drew out some chunks of seaweed that had choked it.

In the time that it took to do this the boat was considerably by the stern. Thick darkness prevailed. All hands had already endured what they felt was the utmost limit. Some of the crew almost lost control of themselves. It was a terrible few minutes, better imagined than described.

We soon had the boat to the surface and the manhead opened. What an experience! While the sun was shining when we went down and the beach lined with soldiers, it was not quite dark with one solitary soldier gazing on the spot where he had seen the boat before going down the last time. He did not see the boat until he saw me standing on the hatch coaming calling for him to stand by to take the line.

The line was struck and the time taken. We had been on the bottom two hours and thirty-five minutes. The candle ceased to burn twenty-five minutes after we went down, showing that we had remained on the bottom two hours and ten minutes after the candle went out. The soldier informed us that we had been given up for lost and that a message had been sent to General Beauregard that a torpedo boat had been lost off Battery Marshall with all hands.

The *USS Housatonic*, a 207-foot-long screw sloop of war, was launched in November 1861 and joined the South Atlantic Blockading Squadron off Charleston the following September.

THE SOLDIER-ARTIST WHO PAINTED THE *HUNLEY*

Conrad Wise Chapman was born on Valentine's Day, 1842, in Washington City (then the name of the U. S. capitol) and raised in Rome, where he studied art under his father, the accomplished painter John Gadsby Chapman. The elder Chapman, whose controversial work, *The Marriage of Pocahontas*, was in the capitol rotunda, had moved from Virginia to Italy to find peace. Despite the ocean separating his studio from the land of his birth, he always maintained a strong identification with the South. His sympathies became even more pronounced with the outbreak of the Civil War.

Conrad, infused with his father's romanticism, sailed from Italy to New York, hoping to enlist in a Virginia regiment. Blocked from reaching Richmond, he instead joined the Third Kentucky Infantry, where his likability and high energy compensated for a lack of soldierly qualities. Chapman, an acquaintance observed, "had not the slightest idea of how to take care of himself . . . he lost, gave away or forgot everything that belonged to him." The one thing Chapman could do was draw, earning the praise of fellow soldiers with his detailed sketchings of everyday camp life.

Chapman got his baptism of fire at Shiloh, receiving wounds serious enough that he required several months' convalesence in Memphis. General Henry A. Wise, a close friend of the family, kept an eye out on the young soldier. Looking to keep him out of harm's way, Wise had Chapman assigned to the 46th Regular Virginia Volunteers as an ordnance sergeant. When the outfit was ordered to Charleston in the fall of 1863, Wise suggested that General P. G. T. Beauregard give the gifted soldier-artist a special assignment: sketching the defenses of Charleston.

Wise's idea was rooted in practicality; the drawings were to accompany a set of maps then being drawn. But Beauregard, a romantic and cultured fellow who also had an eye on his own place in history, saw a more sweeping and powerful use of the artist's talents. Chapman could record for posterity the heroic defense of Charleston. As historian Ben Bassham pointed out more than a century later, Beauregard "liked and recognized the power of pictures."

Between September 16, 1863, and March 5, 1864, Chapman sketched and painted various aspects of the siege of Charleston, including crumbling forts, defiant flags, placid waters, and brilliant sunsets. He worked by day and by night, dodging cannon balls and ignoring pleas to find cover.

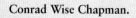

Conrad Wise Chapman.

Chapman's sketch of the *Hunley*.

"Often he sat under a heavy cannonade," recalled one soldier. "He minded it no more than if he had been listening to the post band."

On December 2, 1863, he sketched the *Hunley* cradled on the dock at Mount Pleasant, where the vessel was being refitted and a new crew trained after the accident that had claimed Captain Horace L. Hunley and seven other men. Chapman's pictorial documentation of the submarine came just in time. Eleven weeks later, the *Hunley* disappeared forever during its historic mission against the *Housatonic*.

Chapman left Charleston in April 1864, boarding a blockade runner to visit his ailing mother in Italy. Inside his father's studio he produced a series of paintings based on his sketchings, including the portrait of the *Hunley* that appears on the cover of this book. In his painting of the submarine he evidently was aided by a frontal photograph of the vessel reportedly taken by George Cook on December 3, 1863, the day after Chapman had visited the Mount Pleasant dock. Cook's photograph and Chapman's painting are remarkably alike. All told Chapman created more than thirty paintings; his father added a half-dozen more.

Chapman resisted his parents' attempts to turn his leave into a discharge, ultimately sailing back to the South in the spring of 1865. He landed in Galveston, Texas, just as the war ended. For the next year the young and restless ex-sergeant lived in Mexico with other disgruntled Confederate exiles before beginning a series of travels through the United States and Europe.

In his latter years Chapman was often sick, depressed, and impoverished, but he continued to paint until his death in Hampton, Virginia on December 10, 1910. Today, his wartime canvasses are widely held to be the finest produced by any Confederate artist.

The *Hunley* practices an underwater attack on the *CSS Chicora*. Earlier, five crewmen of the Confederate ironclad ram had volunteered to man the *Hunley*, a decision that cost several of them their lives.

The following day, Beauregard was relieved to learn that that had not been the case. The proof was when the entire crew showed up at headquarters, where the general congratulated them on the results of their endurance test. Dixon, already given sole control over the *Hunley*'s operations, including when it would go out and the choice of target, reassured the Confederate commander that the *Hunley* would engage a Union blockader as soon as conditions warranted it.

On February 5, Dixon responded to a letter from Captain John Cothran, who had been trying without success to get his brave and valued friend to return to duty with Company A of the 21st Alabama.

"You stated my presence was very much needed on your little island," wrote Dixon. "I have no doubt it is, but when I will get there is far more than I am able to tell at present, for beyond a doubt I am fastened to Charleston and its approaches until I am able to blow up some of their Yankee ships. If I wanted to leave here I could not do it, and I doubt very much if an order from General Maury would have any effect towards bringing me back.

"I have been here over three months, have worked very hard, in fact I am working all the time. My headquarters are on Sullivan's Island, and a more uncomfortable place could not be found in the Confederacy. You spoke of being on the front and holding the post of honor. Now, John, make one trip to the beseiged city of Charleston and your post of honor and all danger that threatens Mobile will fade away.

"For the last six weeks I have not been out of the range of shells and often I am forced to go within very close proximity of the Yankee battery. I do not want you and all the company to think that because I am absent from them that mine is any pleasant duty or that I am absent from them because I believe there is any post of honor or fame where there is any danger, I think it must be at Charleston, for if you wish to see war every day and night, this is the place to see it."

On that same day, Alexander and Dillingham were recalled to Mobile for special duty. Alexander's skills were needed immediately to help build a breech-loading repeating cannon. The mysterious Dillingham's assignment is anyone's guess, though it is known that after the war he was still being hunted by Federal authorities.

The new orders were "a terrible blow, both to Dixon and myself, after we had gone through so much together," admitted Alexander. The camaraderie, the excitement, the shared risks, the prospect of being involved in something that was novel and historic—all of this had appealed to him. The transfer practically broke his heart and demoralized the crew when they found out about it the next day. But it also wound up saving the young lieutenant's life.

Taking the places of Alexander and Dillingham were two volunteers from Company A of the South Carolina Light Artillery.

These postwar schematic drawings of the *Hunley* were prepared by William A. Alexander, who directed the vessel's construction in Mobile.

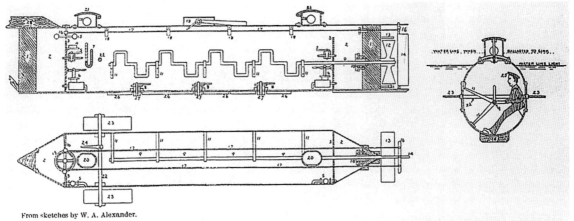

From sketches by W. A. Alexander.

CONFEDERATE STATES SUBMARINE TORPEDO BOAT H. L. HUNLEY. LONGITUDINAL ELEVATION, PLAN, AND TRANSVERSE SECTIONAL VIEWS.

1, The bow and stern castings; 2, water-ballast tanks; 3, tank bulkheads; 4, compass; 5, sea cocks; 6, pumps; 7, mercury gauge; 8, keel-ballast stuffing boxes; 9, propeller shaft and cranks; 10, stern bearing and gland; 11, shaft braces; 12, propeller; 13, wrought ring around propeller; 14, rudder; 15, steering wheel; 16, steering lever; 17, steering rods; 18, rod braces; 19, air box; 20, hatchways; 21, hatch covers; 22, shaft of side fins; 23, side fins; 24, shaft lever; 25, one of the crew turning propeller shaft; 26, cast-iron keel ballast; 27, bolts; 28, butt end of torpedo boom.

One was a corporal named C. F. Carlson; the other was a man whose name is remembered only as Miller. Both were German immigrants.

A minor mystery remains. Who took Alexander's place in the rear hatch as first officer? It certainly wasn't either one of the inexperienced artillery men. The person chosen would have been the most competent of the five transferees from the *Indian Chief*, or possibly the unnamed person who had been part of the four-man group that came to Charleston from Mobile the previous November. In any event, the *Hunley* was quickly back to its normal nine-man complement and, less than two weeks after the departure of Alexander and Dillingham, ready to make history.

The real Rhett Butler? Shipping tycoon George A. Trenholm of Charleston, reputedly the richest man in the South at the outbreak of war, added to his wealth by operating the Confederacy's largest blockade-running companies. Margaret Mitchell is believed to have based the hero of her novel, *Gone with the Wind*, on Tremholm. Blockade running was an extremely profitable business. For example, salt bought for $6.50 a ton in the Bahamas sold for $1,700 in the South.

In early February, a new and inviting target suddenly presented itself to Dixon. Moored about three miles off Rattlesnake Shoal, near Battery Marshall, was one of the finest vessels in the blockading squadron, the *USS Housatonic*.

The screw sloop of war was 207 feet long, thirty-eight feet in the beam, and displaced 1,240 tons. It was built at the Boston Navy Yard and launched on November 29, 1861. The *Housatonic* was commanded by Captain John Pickering and carried a formidable arsenal: a 100-pound and three thirty-pound Parrott rifles, an 11-inch Dahlgren smoothbore, a pair of thirty-two-pound smoothbores, and three howitzers.

The *Housatonic* had been a familiar sight around Charleston for seventeen months, ever since joining the South Atlantic Blockading Squadron in September 1862. It had engaged the Confederate rams *Chicora* and *Palmetto State* in their daring attack in the predawn hours of January 31, 1863, and occasionally landed raiding parties that attacked Charleston's outer defenses. It had also helped capture a number of blockade runners, notably the *Secesh*, the *Neptune*, and the *Princess Royal*. It was while serving in this latter capacity that the *Housatonic* found itself anchored every evening near Rattlesnake Shoal, its boilers and gun crews kept ready in the event an enemy vessel tried to slip past.

Compared to the long-range mission for which the *Hunley* had been preparing, an attack on the *Housatonic* represented no more than a couple of hours of hard cranking each way. All Dixon and

his men needed was a flat sea. On February 17, 1864, after weeks of frightful winds and choppy waves, they got it.

It was early on a Wednesday evening when Dixon and his eight companions wiggled through the hatches into the cold, cramped cylinder that they had become so intimately acquainted with over the last dozen weeks. Drops of melted wax and smudges of smoke could be spotted here and there, the residue from the burning of countless candles. Drops of condensation formed on the damp iron walls. As always, the men stored their canteens of water and parcels of hardtack and dried beef—sustenance for the long night ahead—and took up their individual stations in front of the handcrank.

As they had been doing for some time, the crew set off from Breach Inlet, a nearby passage with a strong current. Earlier, Dixon had arranged with the commander of Battery Marshall "that if he came off safe [from the mission] he would show two blue lights." That is, Dixon would signal by holding two blue lanterns outside his hatchway. The battery would respond with a beacon to guide the submarine back to the narrow mouth of Breach Inlet.

It was a calm, windless night, with the moon punching a hole in the sky. The men inside the *Hunley* cranked steadily for more than an hour, as Dixon did his best to keep them on course. When

Battery Marshall on Sullivan's Island. "My headquarters are on Sullivan's Island," Lieutenant George Dixon wrote a friend in February 1864, "and a more uncomfortable place could not be found in the Confederacy."

February 17, 1864: The
Hunley attacks the
Housatonic.

the *Hunley* was within several hundred yards of its target, Dixon
brought the boat to the surface to make one final observation.
Through the view port he could see the *Housatonic* silhouetted
against the sky, rocking gently at anchor.

It was now about 8:45 P.M. Aboard the *Housatonic*, lookouts
were stationed on the forecastle, gangway, and quarterdeck. From
his spot on the quarterdeck, Acting Master John K. Crosby saw an
object approaching and thought it was a porpoise. The quartermaster took a look through his eyeglass and decided that it was a
school of fish. But as the odd-looking, semisubmersed object kept
steadily approaching, Crosby suddenly thought he recognized the
outline. It appeared to be a Confederate David! He sounded the

alarm and ordered the anchor chain slipped. Officers and crew rushed onto the deck; some began firing rifles and pistols at the onrushing *Hunley*. The order was given to direct cannon fire at it, but by now the submarine was too close to depress the barrels. Within seconds the *Hunley* slammed into the *Housatonic*.

It was as if the *Hunley* had harpooned a great wooden whale. The barbed head of the torpedo jammed into the timbers below the water line on the starboard side, just forward of the mizzen mast. The submarine reversed course, the line playing out from the reel, and then the lanyard was pulled. There was a blast, muffled by the water but severe enough to blow a hole in the vessel's side and send splinters shooting into the sky. A Negro landsman named Theodore Parker was on the lookout directly over where the *Housatonic* was struck. The explosion flung him into the air, killing him instantly.

A survivor described the explosion as "rather sharp," but not louder than the blast from one of the ship's twelve-pound howitzers. "I saw a very large quantity of black smoke, but no column of water, and no flame."

"The explosion started me off my feet, as if the ship had struck hard on the bottom," recalled another survivor. "I saw fragments

As the *Hunley* frantically backs away after implanting a spar torpedo in the hull of its target, the *Housatonic*'s stern blows apart.

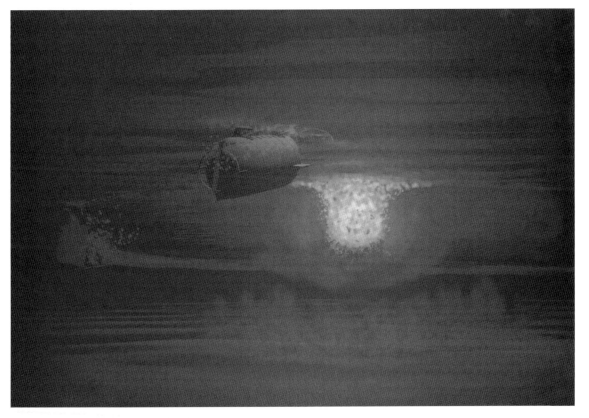

of the wreck going up into the air. I saw no column of water thrown up, no smoke and no flame. There was no sharp report, but it sounded like a collision with another vessel."

"I heard a report like the distant firing of a howitzer," testified Ensign C. H. Craven. "The ship went down by the stern, and about three or four minutes after the stern was submerged, the whole ship was submerged."

Captain Pickering was "seated at the cabin table overhauling a book of charts" when he "heard a confused sound and stir of excitement on deck."

I heard the Officer of the Deck call the Orderly for the transmission of some information. I sprang from the table under the impression that a blockade runner was about. In snatching my cap I found I had taken [assistant surgeon] Dr. Plant's by mistake, who was seated at the table with me at the time. I turned back, got my own, met the orderly at the cabin door, and passed him without waiting to receive his report. On reaching the deck I gave the order to slip and heard for the first time it was a torpedo, I think from the Officer of the Deck. I repeated the order to slip, and gave the order to go astern, and to open fire. I turned instantly, took my double barreled gun, loaded with buckshot, from Mr. Muzzey, my aide and clerk, and jumped up on the horse block on the starboard Quarter, which the First Lieutenant had just left having fired a musket at the Torpedo.

I hastily examined the Torpedo: it was shaped like a large whale boat, about two feet, more or less, under water; its position was at right angles to the ship, bows on, and the bows within two or three feet of the ship's side, about abreast of the mizzen mast, and I supposed it was then finding the torpedo on. I saw two projections or knobs about one third of the way from the bows. I fired at these, jumped down from the horse block, and ran up the port side of the Quarter Deck, as far as the mizzen mast, saying out "Go astern faster." The men were then huddling forward, I would not call them aft to the guns, as they could not be trained until the ship had got some distance from the Torpedo, and they were in a safer place.

I thought of going forward myself to get clear of the Torpedo, but reflecting that my proper station was aft, I remained there, and was blown into the air the next instant from where I stood on the Port side abreast of the mizzen mast. I found myself in the water about where I stood previous to the

explosion amongst broken timbers, the debris of panel work and
planking. I succeeded in getting into the mizzen rigging very
much bruised, and was rescued by a boat. The ship was then
lying over on her Port side, so as to bring her Port Quarters
boat under water she was raised forward and her fore rigging
full of men. The interval of time between the explosion and my
getting into the rigging is unknown to me.

Pickering would later learn that it had taken less than five minutes for his ship to sink.

"As she began to sink the most frightful scenes were wit-
nessed," one survivor recalled. "Men with nothing but their shirts
on were seen struggling in the water, officers were trying to get the
boats loose, while others were mounting the rigging."

Quartermaster John Williams, captain's clerk Charles O.
Muzzey, and John Walsh drowned. Walsh, a fireman from Boston,
"had got safely on the deck," reported one witness, "but ventured
back to save $300, which he had in his bag on the birth deck. Poor
fellow, he never returned." Another unnecesary death was that of
Ensign E. L. Hasiltine. The Connecticut native left the safety of a
launch to jump back on board the *Housatonic* just as it keeled over.
"The last ever seen of him he was floating among the fragments of
the wreck, a corpse."

The *Canandaigua*, stationed nearby, hoisted signals of distress
and rushed to the stricken ship's assistance. The *Housatonic* settled
to the shallow bottom, its masts jutting into the sky. Survivors were
plucked off the rigging, where they had climbed when the deck
went under. From that vantage point at least one seaman, Robert
Flemming, claimed to see a "blue light on the water just ahead of
the *Canadaigua* and on the starboard quarter of the *Housatonic*."
This may have been the signal from the *Hunley* to Battery Marshall
as it fled for the safety of Breach Inlet. It never made it.

A stream of disheveled officers and crew, many of them stark
naked, were hauled aboard the rescue ship and given blankets, hot
coffee, and medical attention. Many were then transferred from the
Canandaigua's crowded decks to the *Wabash*.

The final toll was five men dead, two injured, and—of greatest
significance—one warship sunk. On this chaotic moonlit night off
the coast of South Carolina, the nature of naval warfare had been
changed forever.

The aftermath: The *Hunley* leaves the stricken *Housatonic*.

While Charleston burns in the background, Captain H. M. Bragg raises the U. S. flag over the ruins of Fort Sumter.

Chapter Five

UP FROM THE DEEP

At 11 o'clock on the morning of February 26, 1864, a naval court of inquiry was convened aboard the *USS Wabash* to ascertain the facts of the sinking of the *Housatonic*. Over the next ten days, nineteen witnesses—all officers and men of the *Housatonic*—told what they knew of the attack and their vessel's preparedness. (The proceedings are published for the first time in their entirety as an appendix to this book.)

On March 5, the final day of testimony, the four-man board moved the investigation to the *Canandaigua*, where Captain John Pickering was recovering from his injuries. By now the commander of the *Housatonic* had been all but officially absolved of any negligence in the incident, but the judge advocate and three naval officers sitting in judgment of his actions that night still wanted to hear the skipper's version of events. They emerged satisfied.

"If I had had two minutes to work in," Pickering said ruefully towards the end of the questioning, "I could probably have saved the ship and sunk the torpedo craft."

On March 7, the four-man panel reassembled aboard the *Wabash* and released its conclusions:

First: That the U. S. Steamer *Housatonic* was blown up and sunk by a Rebel torpedo craft on the night of February 17th Last at about 9 o'clock p.m., while lying at an anchor in twenty-four feet of water off Charleston, South Carolina, bearing

E. S. E. and distant from Fort Sumter about 5½ miles. The weather at the time of the occurrence was clear, the night bright and moonlight, wind moderate from the Northward and Westward sea smooth and tide half ebb, the ship's head about W. N. W.

Second: That between 8:45 and 9 o'clock p.m. on said night an object in the water was discovered almost simultaneously by the Officer of the Deck and the lookout stationed at the Starboard cathead, on the starboard bow of the ship about seventy-five or 100 yards distant, having the appearance of a log. That on further and closer observation it presented a suspicious appearance, moved apparently with a speed of three or four knots in the direction of the Starboard Quarter of the ship, exhibiting two protuberances above, and making a slight ripple in the water.

Third: That the strange object approached the ship with a rapidity precluding a gun of the battery being brought to bear upon it, and finally came in contact with the ship on her starboard Quarter.

Fourth: That about one and a half minutes after the first discovery of the strange object the crew were called to Quarters, the cable slipped, and the engine backed.

Fifth: That an explosion occurred about three minutes after the first discovery of the object which blew up the after part of the ship, causing her to sink immediately after to the bottom, with her spar deck submerged.

Sixth: That several shots from small arms were fired at the object while it was alongside or near the ship before the explosion occurred.

Seventh: That the watch on deck, ship and ship's Battery were in all respects prepared for a sudden offensive or defensive movement. That lookouts were properly stationed, and vigilance observed and that Officers and crew promptly assembled at their Quarters.

Eighth: That order was preserved on board and orders promptly obeyed by Officers and crew up to the time of the sinking of the ship.

"In view of the above facts," the report concluded, "the Court have to express the opinion that no further military proceedings are necessary."

With that the investigation into the sinking of the *USS Housatonic* was officially closed. However, to interested parties on both sides, the biggest question remained unanswered.

What had happened to the *Hunley*?

A few hours after the board of inquiry called its initial witnesses, the Confederate command received confirmation of what had been rumored around Charleston ever since the *Hunley* disappeared. On the evening of February 26, a Union picket boat was captured near Fort Sumter. In the course of the prisoners' interrogation it was learned that the ship whose masts were seen jutting out of the water was the *Housatonic*, and that it had been destroyed by an enemy torpedo boat, killing five men. The Federals assumed the protagonist was a David-class vessel, because it had been only partially submerged when it attacked. But General Beauregard knew better. He immediately telegraphed Richmond:

> Prisoners report that it was the U. S. ship of war "Housatonic," twelve guns, which was sunk on night 17th instant by the submarine torpedo boat, Lieutenant Dixon, of Alabama, commanding. There is little hope of safety of that brave man and his associates, however, as they were not captured.

To a besieged city starving for scraps of good news, the sinking of the *Housatonic* was received like a banquet. Charleston papers reported what they knew of the incident and enthusiastically played up its implications.

"The loss of the *Housatonic* caused great consternation in the fleet," observed the *Daily Courier*. "All the wooden vessels are

While maintaining that *Twenty Thousand Leagues Under the Sea* was "entirely a work of the imagination," French author Jules Verne predicted that future wars "may be largely a contest between submarine boats." The French were infatuated with the thought of submarines, with a public subscription helping its navy to build two of them at the turn of the century. The diagram here shows a French submarine of the 1880s, the *Goubet*.

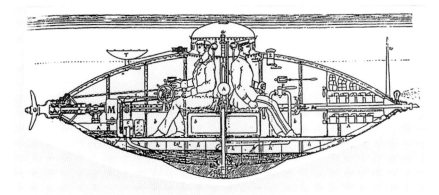

William A. Alexander in 1902.

ordered to keep up steam and go out to sea every night, not being allowed to anchor inside. The picket boats have been doubled and the force in each boat increased.

"This glorious success of our little torpedo boat . . . has raised the hopes of our people, and the most sanguine expectations are now entertained of our being able to raise the siege in a way little dreamed of by our enemy."

This flush of optimism quickly evaporated. It was clear that in a war of attrition, weight of numbers would ultimately squash individual pluck. The North had more of everything. More men, more ships, more shells—and, with the re-election of President Lincoln, who vowed to fight the war through to its conclusion, more resolve. On February 17, 1865, exactly one year to the day that the men of the *Hunley* had demonstrated Southern resoluteness and courage in the waters off Rattlesnake Shoal, the North also had Charleston. "Poor old Charleston," cried one woman joining the evacuation of the ruined city, "after she has withstood the assault for so long and now we must leave her to these wretches."

⟿

On November 27, 1864, nine months after the *Housatonic*'s sinking, Lieutenant W. L. Churchill, in command of the schooner *G. W. Blunt*, sent the following report to Admiral Dahlgren:

The *Housatonic* is very much worm-eaten, as I find from pieces which have been brought up. She is in an upright position; has settled in the sand about five feet, forming a bank of mud and sand around her bed; the mud has collected in her in small quantities. The cabin is completely demolished, as are also all the bulkheads abaft the mainmast; the coal is scattered about her lower decks in heaps, as well as muskets, small arms, and quantities of rubbish.

I tried to find the magazine, but the weather has been so unfavorable and the swell so great that it was not safe to keep a diver in the wreck. I took advantage of all the good weather that I had, and examined as much as was possible.

The propeller is in an upright position; the shaft appears to be broken. The rudder post and rudder have been partly blown off; the upper parts of both are in their proper places, while the lower parts have been forced aft. The stern frame rests upon the rudder post and propeller; any part of it can be easily slung with chain slings, and a powerful steamer can detach each part.

I have also caused the bottom to be dragged to an area of 500 yards around the wreck, finding nothing of the torpedo boat. On the 24th the drag ropes caught something heavy. On sending a diver down to examine it, proved to be a quantity of rubbish. The examination being completed, I could accomplish nothing further, unless it is the intention to raise the wreck or propeller, in which case it will be necessary to have more machinery.

In this circa-1907 postcard view, a policeman stands in front of the *Hunley* monument at Battery Park in Charleston. The eight-foot granite monument was dedicated on May 8, 1899.

With the end of the war fewer than five months off, the U. S. government quickly lost interest in the *Housatonic*. The shattered ship would remain a nuisance to navigation for another nine years, until its rotting superstructure was demolished in the summer of 1873 and the vessel moved to a new position in deeper water off Sullivan's Island. For thirty-six years a buoy marked its location. Then in February 1909, the remaining wreckage was surveyed and dynamited. Boats were finally free to navigate over what remained of its hull. Over the coming years the *Housatonic*'s final resting place was covered by sand and forgotten.

THE TRAGIC TOLL OF THE "PERIPATETIC COFFIN"

This memorial to the men of the *CSS Hunley* is located in Mobile, Alabama, the home town of many of its crew.

As the following list illustrates, service on the *H. L. Hunley* practically guaranteed an early and horrifying death through drowning or asphyxiation. Of the twenty-eight men known to have served on the submarine during its brief existence, only seven managed to survive to describe their experiences to a postwar audience.

Officers

Capt. Horace L. Hunley	Asphyxiated on October 15, 1863
Lt. William A. Alexander	Transferred in 1864
Lt. George E. Dixon	Lost at sea on February 17, 1864
Lt. Charles Hasker	Survived sinking on August 29, 1863; captured in 1863 and exchanged
Lt. James R. McClintock	Transferred in 1863
Lt. Thomas Park	Asphyxiated on October 15, 1863
Lt. John A. Payne	Survived sinking on August 29, 1863; transferred in 1863
Lt. B. A. Whitney	Transferred in 1863

Crew

Henry Beard	Drowned on October 15, 1863
Arnold Becker	Lost at sea on February 17, 1864
Robert Brookbank	Drowned on October 15, 1863
Michael Cane	Drowned on August 29, 1863
C. F. Carlson	Lost at sea on February 17, 1864
F. Collins	Lost at sea on February 17, 1864
Nicholas Davis	Drowned on August 29, 1863
Henry Dillingham	Transferred in 1864
Jeremiah Donivan	Survived sinking on August 29, 1863; transferred in 1863
Frank Doyle	Drowned on August 29, 1863
John Kelly	Drowned on August 29, 1863
John Marshall	Drowned on October 15, 1863
Charles McHugh	Drowned on October 15, 1863
— Miller	Lost at sea on February 17, 1864
Joseph Patterson	Drowned on October 15, 1863
— Ridgeway	Lost at sea on February 17, 1864
C. Simkins	Lost at sea on February 17, 1864
Charles L. Sprague	Survived sinking on August 29, 1863; drowned on October 15, 1863
James A. Wicks	Lost at sea on February 17, 1864
Absolum Williams	Drowned on August 29, 1863

But what of the *Hunley*? After a flurry of rumors that the boat had either sailed into a friendly port or that the crew and the boat had been captured, everybody connected with the enterprise, from General Beauregard to Queenie Bennett, came to accept its obvious fate. The *Hunley* was irretrievably lost at sea, and with it all hands, though nobody could be sure of the exact details of the vessel's demise or the location of the wreck site. In the years immediately following the war, claims of its discovery on the sea floor occasionally appeared in Southern papers, often in conjunction with a story concerning its victim. Typical was this piece in the October 8, 1870, edition of the *Charleston Daily Republican*:

> We all know the fate of the brave *Housatonic*. Brave Dixon guided the torpedo fairly against her, the explosion tore up the great ship's sides, so that she went down with all her crew within two minutes.
>
> The torpedo vessel also disappeared forever from mortal view. Whether she went down with her enemy or whether she drifted out to sea to bury her gallant dead, was never known, and their fate was left till the great day when the sea shall give up her dead.
>
> But within a few weeks past, divers in submarine armor have visited the wreck of the *Housatonic*, and they have found the little torpedo vessel lying by her huge victim, and within are the bones of the most devoted and daring men that ever went to war.

On another occasion Angus Smith, the salvage diver who had twice brought the *Hunley* to the surface in 1863 and was now under contract to remove Confederate wrecks from Charleston harbor, allegedly discovered the submarine lying in excellent condition next to the *Housatonic*. It was Smith's opinion that the boat could be easily raised. These reports simply were not true. But they gave credence to the pervasive belief that the *Hunley* had probably been sucked into the *Housatonic*'s shattered hull by the force of the explosion, drowning its intrepid crew.

The postwar years were filled with hoaxes, fabrications, and wild rumors. Showman P. T. Barnum allegedly offered a staggering $100,000 to anybody who could produce the *Hunley* for display inside his famous New York museum. Meanwhile, the principal characters and bit players associated with the *Hunley*'s history grew old and died off.

The crew of the *USS Holland*, the Navy's first submarine, in June 1901. In the hatch is Lieutenant Harry Caldwell, the commanding officer.

Lieutenant Charles Hasker and Jeremiah Donivan, both of whom survived the sinking of August 29, 1863, made it through the war. Hasker died in 1898, Donivan thirty years later. Lieutenant William McClintock spent the balance of the war mining Mobile Bay; he was blown apart in 1879 testing one of his torpedoes in Boston harbor. Queenie Bennett overcame her grief at Lieutenant Dixon's death by throwing herself into teaching. She married a longtime friend in 1871, moved to Mississippi, and died twelve years later in childbirth. Lieutenant William Alexander emerged as the *Hunley*'s unofficial historian; he and the *Housatonic*'s ill-fated skipper, Captain Pickering, both passed away in 1914.

That year looms large in the history of underwater warfare. For it wasn't until then, a full half-century after the *Hunley* became the first submarine to sink an enemy vessel, that its feat was duplicated. On September 5, 1914, the German *U-21* put a torpedo into the side of the British cruiser *Pathfinder*, killing all but nine of its 268 men.

As evidenced by the success of Germany's fleet of U-boats (shorthand for "underwater boats"), the period between the Civil War and the First World War had been one of tremendous strides in submarine technology, with most of the significant research and development taking place in America. John P. Holland, an Irish schoolteacher with a mechanical bent, came to the United States in 1873 and soon was successfully testing a submersible propelled by an internal combustion engine. His boats also featured advanced control and balance mechanisms. During the Spanish-American War he offered to take his craft to Cuba, where he proposed to single-handedly destroy the enemy fleet.

Although Holland was rebuffed by the War Department, the assistant secretary of the Navy, Theodore Roosevelt, was convinced of the boat's effectiveness. (In 1905 Roosevelt would become the first president to take a submarine ride.) Equally impressed was the hero of Manila Bay, Admiral George Dewey. "I said it then, and I have said it since, that if [the Spanish] had two of those things at Manila, I could never have held it with the squadron I had," Dewey said during a Congressional hearing in 1900. That spring the fifty-three-foot-long *Holland*, fitted with a torpedo tube and dynamite gun, became the first submarine in the U. S. Navy. Holland also built boats for other countries. On the eve of the First World War, Great Britain, France, and Germany all had sizable submarine fleets.

This would have pleased the creators of the *Hunley*. "Since the [Civil War], I have thought over the subject considerable," McClintock wrote in the early 1870s, "and am satisfied that the Power can easily be obtained . . . to make the submarine Boat the most formidable enemy of Marine warfare ever known. . . ."

And the most despised. Whereas the highly individualistic nature of the *Hunley*'s exploits had made its crews into Confederate folk heroes and the object of grudging admiration on the Union side, the anonymous submariners of the new century were accused of plying an unethical trade. The outcry was greatest following the 1915 sinking of the *Lusitania*, the most famous victim of Germany's notorious policy of unrestricted submarine warfare. A single torpedo caused the giant Cunard liner to go to the bottom within eighteen minutes, taking 1,198 men, women, and children to a watery grave. The outrage moved Rudyard Kipling to verse:

> They bear, in place of classic names,
> Letters and numbers on their skin.
> They play their grisly blindfold games
> In little boxes made of tin.

The men aboard a crowded American troop ship nervously scan the water for German submarines as their convoy crosses the Atlantic in 1918.

Kipling rued the absence of romance in modern warfare. Since the Civil War, killing had grown increasingly impersonal and mechanized, a profession better suited to technicians than Galahads. The *Hunley*, for all its heroic overtones, had been an indisputably vital part of that process.

<hr />

The *CSS Hunley* rested unmolested on the ocean floor for well over a century. In the summer of 1980, the American explorer Clive Cussler launched his first of several attempts to find the *Hunley*, whose story had always intrigued him. Cussler, the best-selling author of such books as *Raise the Titanic* and *Inca Gold*, didn't find the submarine, but he did discover what was left of the *Housatonic* about three miles off Sullivan's Island.

Fifteen years later, on May 11, 1995, Cussler announced that, eight days earlier, his search team had found the *Hunley* four miles off Sullivan's Island, resting under thirty feet of water at the approach to Moffitt's Channel.

The only damage appeared to be a rip in the vicinity of the front hatchway. Cussler's opinion was that the *Hunley* survived the explosion, but was victimized by a leak caused by the concussion. "I think they paddled like hell and just didn't make it," he said.

The most experienced divers from the National Park Service spent weeks exploring the site. Their sophisticated high-tech testing verified Cussler's claim. A preliminary corrosion report indicated that a cocoon of mud and silt had helped protect the *Hunley* from severe damage. No weak areas were spotted in the iron hull, which was judged to have at least three more years of life left before serious deterioration set in. According to the diver who actually found the wreck, the *Hunley* was strong enough to withstand the rigors of being lifted from the sea floor.

"It's going to be a piece of cake," said Ralph Wilbanks. "It's going to come up whole, and it's going to look good."

News of the discovery understandably caused a stir among relic hunters, including an immediate black-market offer of $50,000 for a hatch cover. To discourage would-be looters, the exact coordinates of the wreck site remain closely guarded. The site is covered with a cage, set with alarms, and continues to be monitored from shore by an infrared camera. Also, the U. S. Coast Guard enforces a one-square-mile no-travel zone around it. "Get caught messing with it," warned the Sons of Confederate Veterans, which had assisted researcher Mark Newell's twenty-three-year-long hunt for the elusive sub, "and you don't come up for air for five years."

Newell was part of the considerable controversy and back-biting generated by the search for the *Hunley*, a battle waged through conflicting press releases and competing web sites. It had long been Newell's theory that, based on the eyewitness testimony of survivors of the *Housatonic* and a report by Lieutenant Colonel O. M. Dantzler, commander of Battery Marshall, Dixon's pre-arranged signals of a blinking blue light had been observed some time after the attack. This meant that the *Hunley* had not been dragged down with its victim, but rather had been able to steal away from the scene. But at what point in the ocean had the fleeing *Hunley* finally gone down? And why? Newell didn't figure to be able to answer the second question, at least not until he had answered the first.

Writer Christopher Chase was involved in Newell's odyssey from the beginning. He gave the following account of it in *Blue & Gray Magazine*:

> Simple observation led Newell to the probable location of the submarine in 1973. It is known that Lt. George Dixon took

HOW MANY SINKINGS?

Private Arthur P. Ford.

The actual number of sinkings suffered by the *CSS Hunley* continues to be debated. During the submarine's six months at Charleston, it was an article of faith among many civilians and garrison troops that Horace Hunley's unlucky diving machine had claimed several crews, including one or two in Mobile, even before its final fatal mission against the *Housatonic*. In this recollection by Arthur P. Ford, a private serving with Buist's Battery, South Carolina Artillery, no less than six fatal accidents are described, double the number that historians have documented.

As I was standing on the bank of the Stono River, I saw the boat passing along the river, where her builder, H. L. Hundley, had brought her for practice. I watched her as she disappeared around a bend of the river, and little thought of the fearful tragedy that was immediately to ensue. She made an experimental dive, stuck her nose in the mud, and drowned her entire crew. Her career was such an eventful one that I record what I recollect of it.

She was built in Mobile by Hundley, and brought on to Charleston in 1863. She was of iron, about twenty feet long, four feet wide, and five feet deep—in fact, not far from round, as I have seen it stated; and equipped with two fins, by which she could be raised or lowered in the water. . . . She was worked by a hand propeller, and equipped with water tanks, which could be filled or emptied at pleasure, and thus regulate her sinking or rising. The first experiment with her was made in Mobile Bay, and she went down all right with her crew of seven men, but did not come up, and every man died, asphyxiated, as no provision had been made for storing a supply of air.

As soon as she was raised, she was brought to Charleston, and a few days after her acceptance by General Beauregard, Lieutenant Payne, of the Confederate Navy, volunteered with a crew of six men to man her and attack the Federal fleet off Charleston. While he had her at Fort Johnson, on James Island, and was making preparations for the attack, one night as she was lying at the wharf the swell of a passing steamer filled her, and she went to the bottom, carrying with her and drowning the six men. Lieutenant Payne happened to be near an open manhole at the moment, and thus he alone escaped.

Notwithstanding the evidently fatal characteristics of this boat, as soon as she was raised another crew of six men volunteered under Payne and took charge of her. But only a week afterwards an exactly similar accident happened while she was alongside the wharf at Fort Sumter, and only Payne and two of his men escaped.

H. L. Hundley, her builder in Mobile, now believed that the crews did not understand how to manage the *"Fish,"* and came on to Charleston to see if he could not show how it should be done. A Lieutenant Dixon, of Alabama, had made several successful experiments with the boat in Mobile Bay, and he also came on, and was put in charge, with a volunteer crew, and made several successful dives in the harbor. But one day, the day on which I saw the boat, Hundley himself took it into Stono River to practice her crew. She went down all right, but did not come up, and when she was searched for, found and raised to the surface, all of her crew were dead, asphyxiated as the others had been.

After the boat was brought up to Charleston, several successful experiments were made with her, until she attempted to dive under the Confederate receiving ship *Indian Chief,* when she got entangled with an anchor chain and went to the bottom, and remained there until she was raised with every one of her crew dead, as were their predecessors.

No sooner had she been raised than a number of men begged to be allowed to give her another trial, and Lieutenant Dixon was given permission to use her in an attack on the USS *Housatonic,* a new gunboat that lay off Beach Inlet on the bar, on the condition that she should not be used as a submarine vessel, but only on the surface with a spar torpedo. On February 17, 1864, Lieutenant Dixon, with a crew of six men, made their way with the boat through the creeks behind Sullivan's Island to the inlet. The night was not very dark, and the *Housatonic* easily could be perceived lying at anchor, unmindful of danger. The *"Fish"* went direct for her victim and her torpedo striking the side tore a tremendous hole in the *Housatonic,* which sank to the bottom in about four minutes. But as the water was not very deep her masts remained above water, and all of the crew, except four or five saved themselves by climbing and clinging to them. But the *"Fish"* was not seen again.

his submarine out of Breach Inlet each time he launched an attack on the blockade fleet. The reason is obvious enough even today. As the tides begin to turn from slack to ebb in the Back Bay behind Sullivan's Island, a huge volume of water forces its way through Breach Inlet. The strong current must have provided a free ride to the crew of eight who sat behind Dixon at a hand crank used to propel the craft. As the tides turn again to flood, the incoming current is not as strong. Clearly the Back Bay filled from other sources that provided the incoming tide with readier access. The obvious next choice was was the huge entrance to Charleston Harbor on the south end of Sullivan's Island. In escaping the scene of the attack, the crew of the *Hunley* would have taken full advantage of their knowledge of local tides. Newell believed that Dixon signaled Battery Marshall from a location along a route from the wreck of the *Housatonic* to Charleston Harbor's mouth, where the strongest tidal flow would have lent speed to their escape.

The route led to Maffitt's Channel, which was closed in 1880 when massive granite jetties were built to aid navigation. Dives made in the area proved that the channel had silted in. These conditions meant that the area had to be searched with sensitive ship-towed metal detectors if the *Hunley* were to be found.

After several abortive attempts, this was not accomplished until the summer of 1994, when Newell succeeded in encouraging Clive Cussler to support a search of the area. Cussler had made brief and unsuccessful searches in 1980 and 1981 for the submarine. By 1994, Newell was completing a Ph.D. in underwater archaeology at St. Andrews University in Scotland.

The project searched almost fifty square miles of ocean off Charleston Harbor's mouth in the first weeks of August 1994. In the last days of the field work, an object matching the size and mass of the *Hunley* was found in the spot Newell had predicted, in the approaches to Maffitt's Channel, one of several "targets" found in the general area.

A day was spent in September 1994 carefully probing and mapping the object with volunteers who were able to determine that the object was within thirty to forty feet long, within five feet wide and had a curved upper surface. Newell had been authorized by the federal government to dig small test pits in order to uncover and hopefully identify any objects found during the search. Rather than prematurely disturb a possible national treasure, Newell decided to examine the object with high resolution sonar in the spring of 1995.

The time-consuming conduct of such non-invasive science evidently tested the patience of the university's partner. In May of 1995, a month before sonar testing was scheduled, Clive Cussler ordered his own divers to excavate targets found in the Maffitt's Channel area, revealing the *Hunley*.

"Clearly," concluded Chase, "Cussler's intention was to pre-empt Newell's confirmation of the discovery and reap the benefits of the publicity for himself."

Newell wasn't the only one with a bone to pick with Cussler. Concurrent with Cussler's 1980 discovery of the *Housatonic*, underwater archaeologist Edward Lee Spence of Charleston filed papers in Federal District Court to secure ownership and salvage rights to the *Housatonic* and the *Hunley*, claiming to have discovered both ten years earlier. For the next fifteen years Spence vigorously defended his claim in the press and in the courts. On September 14, 1995, four months after Cussler's announcement that he had found the submarine, Spence donated ownership rights to the *Hunley* to the State of South Carolina. In early 1997, the official state Hunley Commission rejected Spence's claim and announced that Cussler had planned and supported the expedition that located the *Hunley*.

This Confederate Medal of Honor was awarded March 25, 1991, to the final crew of the *Hunley* by the Sons of Confederate Veterans.

Since then, divers from the National Park Service and scientists from the University of South Carolina have thoroughly measured, investigated, and recorded the wreck site. A federal oversight committee was formed to review recovery proposals, which basically boiled down to three options:

- Leave the *Hunley* undisturbed, protecting the site in perpetuity.
- Conduct an underwater archaeological survey and other testing, then rebury the vessel and protect the site.
- Recover the *Hunley* and conduct the necessary archaeological and scientific studies and conserve the vessel for future generations.

In the summer of 1999, the last option seemed to be the best choice. To that end the Hunley Commission accepted a proposal by the Charleston Museum to serve as the *Hunley*'s permanent home. The challenge continues to be in finding the estimated $15 million to raise, restore, and curate the boat. This includes the cost of building a special recovery tank to hold the submarine for years of slow chemical process stabilization and cleaning.

It appears that the many questions about the *Hunley*, its crew, and their fatal last mission will be answered—if not soon, then soon enough. What has never been questioned was the resolve of this plucky band of submariners, or what drove them to volunteer their lives.

Just days before his death, Dixon composed a letter to his former company commander. In ending this, the last letter he would ever write, he spoke of his motivation, a lofty blend of patriotism and immortality. The young lieutenant's words could serve as the *Hunley*'s epitaph.

"Charleston and its defenders will occupy the most conspicuous place in the history of the war," said Dixon, "and it shall be as much glory as I shall wish if I can inscribe myself as one of its defenders."

The *Hunley* today lies partially buried in sand, six fathoms deep.

A contemporary sketch shows the "Destruction of Housatonic by a rebel torpedo."

THE *HUNLEY* RESURFACES

On the clear, warm morning of August 8, 2000, the first submarine to sink an enemy sea vessel in battle resurfaced after spending the last 136-and-a-half-years on what submariners call "eternal patrol."

"Gone from the waters off Charleston Harbor, South Carolina, were the enemy Federal blockade ships and the black, smoke-filled air of a nighttime sea battle," wrote Eric Ethier in *Civil War Times*. "Present were hundreds of eager onlookers gathered under a sunny sky on shore and on dozens of motorboats and sailing vessels. And when the giant crane mounted on the 600-ton barge *Karlissa B.* gently lifted the legendary sub from its watery grave, the excited audience erupted in cheers. A new kind of history had been made."

That "new kind of history" referred to the recovery methods employed in safely raising, housing, and examining the *H. L. Hunley*, which archaeologists and historians universally lauded as one of the most significant historical excavations ever.

The submarine's resurfacing was delayed several months as the recovery team worked out a plan to bring the Confederate "fish-boat" to the surface without irreversibly damaging it. First, two suction piles were placed off the bow and the stern of the *Hunley*. These suction piles, which were buried about twelve feet below the seafloor, were used to support the specially designed steel box truss that was then lowered over the submarine. An area was excavated in the sand underneath the *Hunley*, allowing divers to loop synthetic straps and foam-filled sacks around the hull, securely cradling the submarine inside the box truss. In a move that created some controversy, the hull bracket holding the spar in place was unbolted to facilitate the sub's recovery.

Described as "a dolphin in a sling," the *Hunley* broke the surface to a cacophony of whistles, foghorns, shouts, and cheers and was lifted onto a recovery barge, which then made its way on a three-hour, fifteen-mile journey to a pier on the old Charleston Naval Base. There it was transferred to a giant cold-water storage tank inside a nearby high-tech laboratory, the Warren Lasch Conservation Center.

"It's much smaller than I thought," remarked Clive Cussler. "It's only three-foot (wide) by four-foot (tall). Those guys onboard couldn't have been over 5-foot-2."

To gain access to the sub's interior, several plates from the hull—each about 33-inches wide—were removed. Then began the painstaking task of sifting through the sediment that filled the *Hunley*, mud that "had the appearance and consistency of raw cookie dough," according to one reporter. "Coaxing the delicate remains of a crewman's hat from the cement-hard encrustation was like trying to get wet tissue paper out of rock," said Shea McLean, one of several archaeologists who spent several months carefully uncovering skeletal remains and personal belongings of the crew.

The most exciting find was Lt. George Dixon's good-luck piece from his sweetheart, Queenie Bennett—the twenty-dollar gold coin that had saved his life at Shiloh and was rumored to have accompanied him on his final mission. The romantic legend became fact when Maria Jacobson, a Danish nautical archaeologist nicknamed "Goldfinger" for her knack in discovering precious metals in digs all over the world, poked about in the muck one day and suddenly fingered a round, slightly warped object. "I think I've got it," she said.

Goldfinger had done it once again, finding the most eagerly anticipated artifact of the *Hunley* excavation. Before armed guards could hustle the shiny coin to a safe, Jacobsen had an opportunity to spend some time contemplating it. It was an 1860 Lady Liberty coin, its surface dented in one spot and worn smooth in others—evidently the result of Dixon rubbing it for good luck. On its reverse side was an ornate inscription:

Shiloh
April 6ᵗʰ 1862
My life Preserver
G.E.D.

One discovery raised more questions than it answered. Amid the muck, a copper medallion bearing a soldier's name, Ezra Chamberlin, was found. These privately purchased "dog tags" were quite common during the Civil War. The trouble was, Chamberlin was a Union soldier who had fought with Company K of the Seventh Regiment of Connecticut Volunteers. What was his medallion doing on the *Hunley*? Speculation ran rampant. Some thought Chamberlin was a defector who had joined the *Hunley*'s crew. Others said he was prisoner of war who had been forced into submarine service. Researchers came across a Private Ezra Chamberlin who had apparently been killed during the 1863 assault on Morris Island, but further digging revealed that the Yankee soldier's mother had been denied a military pension because her son's body had never been found. The true story of Ezra Chamberlin's medallion will probably never be known, though the most logical explanation is that it was picked up by one of the *Hunley*'s crew members and simply worn as a souvenir.

Likewise, the puzzle of exactly why the *Hunley* sank shortly after attacking the *Housatonic* remains unsolved. Scientists found no indications of plate buckling or hull breaches, which would suggest the submarine cracked from the pressure of exploding its torpedo so close to its target. The theory that small arms fired from the *Housatonic* had penetrated the conning tower (wounding or killing Lt. Dixon in the process), thus causing the *Hunley* to flood and plunge to the sea floor, took its own hit when no bullet holes showed up in the tower or Dixon's skull. Scientists determined that any gashes they did find in the hull did not happen contemporaneously with the sinking.

There was one intriguing scenario suggested by the mangled condition of the propeller shroud and the location of the *Hunley*'s rudder. The port side of the shroud was completely gone while the starboard side showed several gashes—an indication, perhaps, that the *Hunley* had been clipped by the *Canandaigua*'s propeller as the massive Union flagship sailed to the rescue of the *Housatonic*. The *Hunley*'s rudder was found under the hull, an unusual spot for it, but not so odd had it been dangling loose as the suddenly disabled submarine crashed out-of-control into the sea floor.

Scientific sleuthing also suggests the crew of the *Hunley* did not drown but rather died of anoxia, the lack of oxygen to the brain. Tiny stalactites were found hanging from the ceiling of the crew compartment. These icicles of calcium are formed from dripping water, either from condensation or pinhole leaks, but they do not form underwater. This indicated that the sub's interior had remained dry for some time after its sinking, meaning the men had not drowned in some catastrophic flooding of the vessel. Also, the skeletons of most of the crew members were found at their duty stations: Dixon in the conning tower, the other men on the bench opposite the hand crank. "Had the interior been filled with water immediately," observed Charleston journalist Brian Hicks, "the bodies would have floated to the same, highest spot in the submarine, resulting in a single, massive pile of bones in one part of the crew compartment as the remains settled."

The combination of clues has led some to hypothesize that the *Hunley*'s crew stayed at their battle stations while their oxygen slowly, imperceptibly, gave out. The end would have been mercifully swift and painless. The men would have gradually grown groggy, passed out, and then suffocated. But what put the men and their vessel in this position? Had the *Hunley* been sent plummeting to the sandy sea floor by collision or concussion? Or had Dixon submerged the *Hunley* voluntarily and for some reason or another—mechanical failure, human error—been unable to bring it back up to the surface? Some have theorized that the exhausted crew simply lost track of time underwater and gradually succumbed to anoxia as the submarine made its way back home. At this point, no one can really say with absolute authority what happened in the final minutes of the *Hunley*'s final mission. Scientific research will continue for years. In the end, the guess of an unschooled tourist may be as good as the hypothesis of the most experienced archaeologist analyzing data.

Today, visitors are welcomed inside the Warren Lasch Conservation Center, the *Hunley*'s final stop. Tourists can purchase mousepads, key chains, coffee mugs, and cropped tees, even a replica of Lt. Dixon's gold coin, all officially licensed by the Friends of the *Hunley*, the organization funding the ongoing preservation and research efforts. Or they can simply drink in the drama, leaving with nothing but admiration and wonder over this painstakingly reconstructed tale of courage, ingenuity—and mystery.

RICHARD BAK
SEPTEMBER, 2002
DEARBORN, MICHIGAN

THE OFFICIAL NAVAL COURT OF INQUIRY INTO THE SINKING OF THE *HOUSATONIC*

Feby. 26/64

Proceedings of a Naval Court of Inquiry convened on board the U.S. Steam Frigate *Wabash* off Charleston S. C. on Friday, February 26th, 1864 in pursuance of the following order from Rear Admiral John A. Dahlgren, commanding South Atlantic Blockading Squadron.

Flag Ship *John Adams*
off Morris Island S. C.
February 22, 1864

Captain J. F. Green
Captain Jno. DeCamp
Commander J. L. Williamson

Gentlemen:

You are constituted a Court of Inquiry to ascertain the facts of the recent disaster that befell the U.S. Steam Ship *Housatonic*, through the agency of a Rebel Torpedo.

Which you will state with your opinion thereon.

Lieut. Young of the Marine Corps will act as Judge Advocate.

Please to signify to me as soon as possible, what officers and men may be required for evidence, so that they may not be sent away when needed.

Respectfully
Your Obdt. Servt.
Jno. A. Dahlgren
Rear Admiral Comdg.
S.AB. Squadron

U. S. Frigate *Wabash*
off Charleston, S. C.
Friday, Feby. 26, 1864

The Court met at 11 o'clock A.M. pursuant to the foregoing order: Present

Capt. Joseph F. Green U.S.N.
Capt. John DeCamp U.S.N.
Comdr. J. L. Williamson U.S.N. and
2nd Lieut. Jas. B. Young, U.S.M.C. Judge Advocate

The court was then duly sworn according to law by the Judge Advocate, and the Judge Advocate duly sworn according to law, by the President of the Court.

The order convening the Court was then read aloud by the Judge Advocate. Acting Master John H. Crosby was then called and duly sworn according to law.

Question by Judge Advocate. Please state your name and rank in the service of the United States.

Answer. John H. Crosby, Acting Master.

Question by Judge Advocate. What vessel have you last been attached to, and how long have you been so attached?

Answer. The U.S. Steam Sloop *Housatonic*. I have been attached to her since the second day of September 1862.

Question by Judge Advocate. Please state all you know of the recent disaster that befell the *Housatonic*.

Answer. I took the deck at 8 P.M. on the night of February 17th, about 8:45 P.M., I saw something on the water, which at first looked to me like a porpoise coming up to the surface to blow. It was about 45 to 100 yards from us on our starboard beam. The ship heading NW by W. ½ W at the time, the wind two or three points on the starboard bow. At that moment, I called the Quartermaster's attention to it asking him if he saw nothing but a tide ripple on the water. Looking again within an instant I saw it was coming towards the ship very fast. I gave orders to beat to Quarters, slip the chain and back the engine, the orders being executed immediately. At this time the officer of the Forecastle, Acting Master's Mate L. A. Corinthwait, came aft and reported seeing this object on the water. At the same time I informed the Captain that I saw something on the water coming towards the ship very fast, but could not make out what it was. About this time the Executive Officer Lieut. Higginson, came up on the bridge and asked me what I had seen. I told him I saw a swash on the water, but could not tell what it was. Capt. Pickering then came on deck, gave orders to slip the chain and back the engine, and asked me what I had seen. I told him I saw something on the water that looked like a tide ripple or a porpoise, but I could not tell what it was. I then jumped down off the bridge, the Executive Officer having taken the deck, and started to go forward to see that the chain had been slipped. As I was going forward I looked over the side; I saw what appeared to me a plank sharp at both ends, about 20 feet from the ship's side; I went forward, and, as I was coming aft again, the explosion took place. After I gave the order to go to quarters several muskets were fired at it, and when it was close alongside Capt. Pickering fired his gun at it. I don't think it was over 2½ or 3 minutes from the time I first saw the object on the water until it struck, just abaft the mizzen mast, on the starboard side and the explosion took place. The order was then given to clear away all boats. I was abreast the engine room hatch on the starboard side when the explosion took place. I jumped over to the port side and into the dingy and gave orders to the men around to help me clear it away. I cut the falls and while cleaning it away the Ship rolled heavily to Port, and the Dingy swamped. The ship commenced filling as soon as the explosion took place, and was full of water and on the bottom when she lurched heavily to Port, all this occupying about a minute or a minute and a half. After the Dingy swamped I jumped into the rigging, went up into the main top and down on the starboard side, and took four men, cleaned away the third cutter, and started to pick up men who were in the water; after I had picked up the men I pulled towards the ship again, took two men off some pieces of the deck that lay close to the ship's quarter. At this time I heard Capt. Pickering's voice in the Port mizzen rigging: he told me to take him out of the rigging and pull for the *Canandaigua*, he afterwards said pick up all the men and Officers you can find in the water who are in danger, before you come for me. I obeyed his orders then took him out of the rigging and started for the *Canandaigua*. When I picked these men up in the water, all the rest of the men and Officers had got into the fore and main rigging. They were unable to clear away the launches, as they were in iron cranes and could not be got out in time enough. The 4th Cutter and Dingy were swamped when she lurched to Port. Before I got to the *Canandaigua* she had slipped and was standing towards the wreck. I went alongside of the *Canandaigua*, put my men aboard, got a fresh crew and started back for the wreck, with boats from the *Canandaigua* and took two boat loads of men to her.

Question by the Court. State the number and stations of lookouts, and also of Officers on deck on duty at the time the strange object was discovered approaching the *Housatonic*.

Answer. There were six lookouts stationed one on each cathead, gangway and quarter; the Quartermaster was on the Quarterdeck; and Officer on the Forecastle, and the Officer of the deck on the bridge.

Question by the Court. Describe particularly its apparent dimensions, shape and appearance when you saw it on going forward to see if the cable had been slipped.

Answer. It looked to me about 25 or 30 feet long, and between 3 and 4 feet wide, like a whale boat upset, and there was a raised appearance about the center of it, which made a ripple in the water.

Question by the Court. Why did you give orders to back the Engine? And had the ship sternboard when the explosion took place?

Answer. I gave the order to back the engine to avoid the danger of fouling the propeller with the slip rope. I think she had very little stern board when the explosion took place.

Question by the Court. State in what direction with reference to the keel of the ship the strange object approached the ship.

Answer. When I first discovered it, it was approaching at right angles to the keel, and head pointed amidships: as it neared the ship I thought it would strike near the mizzen mast, though it was still approaching at right angles to the keel.

Question by the Court. Could a gun or guns have been brought to bear on the object at any time after its discovery? and were any fired at it? if nay, state the reasons there were not.

Answer. No gun could have been brought to

bear upon the object because there was not time to train one, in consequence of its moving so rapidly towards the ship; therefore, no gun was fired.

Question by the Court. What was the state of the *Housatonic*'s battery, and the watch on deck in regard to readiness for action at the time referred to in the preceding question?

Answer. The Battery was all cast loose; the 30 pdr. Parrott gun on the foremast was pivoted to Port; the 100 pdr. Parrott gun abaft the foremast was pivoted to Starboard; the XI in. gun between the main and mizzen masts was pivoted to Port; the balance of the guns were broad side guns, and were cast loose with side tackles hooked in the fighting bolts. There were four men stationed at the starboard chain ready to slip it if required; there were six lookouts stationed armed with rifles, and the balance of the watch at the guns armed as at quarters.

Question by the Court. When Capt. Pickering fired with his guns into the Torpedo where was he standing?

Answer. I think he was standing on the starboard horse block which is about 15 or 20 feet abaft the mizzen mast.

Question by the Court. From what you saw could you form any idea of how the torpedo vessel was propelled? If so, state how it was propelled.

Answer. I could not form any idea.

Question by the Court. When you took Capt. Pickering out of the mizzen rigging after the explosion, what was his physical condition?

Answer. He seemed to be very much exhausted. I don't think he could have held on much longer.

Question by the Court. State particularly all the effects of the explosion which came under your observation.

Answer. The explosion started me off my feet, as if the ship had struck hard on the bottom. I saw fragments of the wreck going up into the air. I saw no column of water thrown up, no smoke and no flame. There was no sharp report, but it sounded like a collision with another vessel.

Question by the Court. State the force and direction of the wind and tide, and state of the weather on the night and at the time the explosion took place.

Answer. The wind was about NW by N. Force 3. The tide was setting to N.E., about one knot per hour; the weather was clear, very bright moonlight.

Question by the Court. Were order and discipline preserved on board the *Housatonic*? and were the Officers and crew prompt in obeying orders up to the time of her sinking?

Answer. Order and discipline were preserved. The Officers and crew were prompt in obeying all orders.

Question by the Court. About how soon after the discovery of the object approaching the ship was the cable slipped, and the propeller in motion?

Answer. The cable was slipped in about 1½ minutes, and the propeller was turning at the same time.

Question by the Court. Were any other precautions observed on board of the *Housatonic* than those you have already stated to discover the approach of an enemy? If yes, state them.

Answer. There were not.

Question by the Court. What orders had you received as Officer of the Deck in case of the approach of an enemy?

Answer. I had orders whenever I saw anything that looked suspicious to beat the gong for Quarters immediately, slip the chain and back the engine to clear the ship of the slip ropes; and to call the Captain at the same time.

Question by the Court. Was anything omitted to be done that could have been done to the save the ship?

Answer. There was nothing omitted; everything was done that could have been done.

The testimony having been read to the witness and approved by him he then withdrew.

At 2:10 P.M. the Court took a recess. The Court re-assembled at 2:30 P.M. all the members and the Judge Advocate present.

Ensign C. H. Craven was then called and duly sworn according to law.

Question by Judge Advocate. Please state your name and rank in the service of the United States.

Answer. Charles H. Craven, Ensign.

Question by Judge Advocate. What vessel have you been last attached to, and how long have you been so attached?

Answer. The U.S. Steam Sloop *Housatonic*, where I reported January 12, 1864.

Question by Judge Advocate. Please state all you know in relation to the disaster that befell the *Housatonic*.

Answer. I was in my room about 9 P.M. on the

Using handguns, the crew of the *Housatonic* futilely tries to defend their ship against the *Hunley*.

evening of Feb. 17th, when I heard the Officer of the Deck give the order "Call all hands to Quarters"; I went on deck and saw something in the water on the Starboard side of the ship making towards the ship about 30 feet off and the Captain and Executive Officer were firing at it. It looked to me like a water logged plank, with something standing up in the center of it about 18 inches apparently; I was then standing by the after pivot guns port on the Starboard side, abreast of the Wardroom hatch. I heard the order given by the Captain, I supposed, to slip the chain and ring three bells to back her. I fired two shots at her with my revolver as she was standing towards the ship as soon as I saw her, and a third shot where she was almost under the counter, having to lean over the port to fire it. I then went to my division, which is the second, and consists of four broadside 32 pdr. Guns in the waist, and tried with the Captain of No. 6 gun to train it on this object, as she was backing from the ship, and about 40 or 50 feet off then. I had nearly succeeded, and was about to pull the lock string when the explosion took place. I was jarred and thrown back and the topsail sheet bitts, which caused me to pull the lock string and the hammer fell on the primer but without sufficient force to explode it. I replaced the primer and was trying to catch sight of the object in order to train the gun again upon it, when I found the water was ankle deep on deck by the main mast. I then went and assisted in clearing away the 2nd Launch. The Gig and 3rd Cutter had already been cleared away, had picked up some men and pulled for the Canandaigua. I tried to clear away the Launch, but though both falls were cut the crutches and cranes held the boat and I could not get her into the water. Seeing the Gig and 3rd Cutter were pulling towards the Canandaigua, I assisted some men who were in the water into the launch and waited for the Canandaigua to come up. While waiting, I went aft with James Timmerman, Captain of the Fore top, on the ridge rope, and groped around in hopes of finding Mr. Hazeltine, who I had heard was in the 4th Cutter. I could not find him, but saw shelves filled with crockery and glasses drifting about, some of which I recognized as belonging to the Cabin. I found our hammock under the 4th Cutter, and then went forward to the 2nd Launch, and found two men drowning, holding on to the boom cover, stretched between the foremast and smoke stack. I got them into the launch and then waited

until Lieut. Manley came alongside in one of the Canandaigua's boats.

Question by the Court. State the number of lookouts, and also of Officers on deck on duty usually.

Answer. There was one lookout on each cathead, gangway, and quarter, the Officer of the Deck aft; a Master's Mate on the forecastle; the Quartermaster on the Quarterdeck.

Question by the Court. Describe particularly the apparent dimensions, shape and appearance of this object when you saw it.

Answer. What I saw above water appeared to be the size of a man's head; and, on a level with the water, it seemed to be twelve feet long, and looked like the keel of a whaleboat capsized.

Question by the Court. Had the ship stern board when the explosion took place?

Answer. I do not know.

Question by the Court. State in what direction with reference to the keel of the ship the strange object approached the ship when you saw her.

Answer. Making about 45° with the keel of the ship, approaching the counter, coming from forward.

Question by the Court. What interval of time was there between your first seeing the torpedo craft and the explosion?

Answer. I should think not more than three minutes.

Question by the Court. Could a gun or guns have been brought to bear on the object at any time after you discovered it, and were any fired at it? if nay, state the reasons there were not.

Answer. I don't think any gun could have been brought to bear after I came on deck; the one I attempted to train on it, I depressed the muzzle as much as possible and though it would go over a very little, but intended to fire thinking the shot might strike something under the water. I don't think any other gun could have been trained on it, as the ship sank so quickly.

Question by the Court. How long after the explosion occurred did the ship sink?

Answer. I should think she settled on the bottom in about five minutes after the explosion.

At 3:35 P.M. the Court adjourned until 10 a.m. Saturday, February 24th, 1864, or as soon thereafter as practicable.

11 A.M. Saturday, Feb. 24, 1864.

The Court met pursuant to adjournment: Present

Capt. Jos. F. Green
Capt. John De Camp
Comdr. J.C. Williamson
2nd Lieut. Jas. B. Young, Judge Advocate

The record of yesterday's proceedings were read over and approved. Ensign C. H. Craven was then recalled.

Question by the Court. State particularly all the effects of the explosion that came under your observation.

Answer. At the time of the explosion, I was training a gun and did not notice what the immediate effects were; but, feeling the water about my feet, I started forward and found the ship was sinking very rapidly aft. Almost immediately she gave a lurch to Port, and settled on the bottom. Afterwards, in looking about aft for the body of Mr. Hazeltine, I saw that the Starboard side of the Quarter deck abaft the mizzen mast, and the furniture of the Wardroom and Cabin were floating within the ridge rope so that I supposed the whole starboard side of the ship abaft the mizzen mast was blown off. I heard a report like the distant firing of a howitzer. The ship went down by the stern, and about three or four minutes after the stern was submerged, the whole ship was submerged.

Question by the Court. What was the state of the weather on the night and at the time the explosion took place?

Answer. The sky was clear, with few clouds; little or no sea on; the weather good and the moon and stars shone clearly; a moderate wind from Northward and Westward.

Question by the Court. Were order and discipline preserved on the *Housatonic*, and were the Officers and crew promptly obeying orders from the time you came on deck until the ship sank?

Answer. As far as I could see order and discipline were preserved; and the Officers and crew obeyed all orders.

Question by the Court. Do you know at what time the cable was slipped, and the propeller put in motion? If so, state it.

Answer. I do not know.

Question by the Court. What was the state of preparation of your Division for action on the night and previous to the explosion?

Answer. The guns were cast loose and provided, the side tackles led out and hooked in the training bolts; No. 6 gun on both sides loaded with solid shot; No. 5 gun on both sides with blank cartridges. A five and ten second fuze shell at each gun on deck. The watch on deck belonging to the Division sleeping near their guns; the Division ready to fire at any time the order might be given.

Question by the Court. What was the nearest land to the *Housatonic*, and about how far distant?

Answer. Long Island—distant I should think within five miles.

Question by the Court. Was anything to your knowledge omitted to be done, that could have been done to save the *Housatonic*?

Answer. Nothing.

Question by the Court. What was the interval of time between your first seeing and firing at the Torpedo craft, and when you saw it at forty or fifty feet from the ship.

Answer. About three minutes.

The testimony having been read over to the witness and pronounced correct by him he withdrew.

At 12:30 P.M. the Court took a recess. At 12:55 P.M. the Court re-assembled, all the Members and the Judge Advocate present.

Acting Master J. W. Congdon was then called and duly sworn according to law.

Question by Judge Advocate. Please state your name and rank in the service of the United States.

Answer. Joseph W. Congdon, Acting Master.

Question by Judge Advocate. What vessel have you been last attached to, and how long have you been so attached?

Answer. The U.S. Steam Sloop *Housatonic*, since June 28th, 1862.

Question by Judge Advocate. Please state all you know in relation to the late disaster that befell the *Housatonic*.

Answer. At about 8:45 P.M. on the 17th of February I hear the Office of the Deck call out "Quarters." I went on deck and went forward to slip the chain; when I got forward I found the chain had been unshackled and was entirely clear. I went aft to the bridge, my station at Quarters. Just before I got there I heard them firing muskets at something over the side, and looked over the side to see what they were firing at and saw something that looked like a water logged timber, touching the starboard side of the ship; I was standing in the middle of the starboard after-pivot gun's port, and this object was about eight feet abaft of where I was standing. I drew my revolver, but, before I could fire, the explosion took place. I immediately went forward and ordered the Launches to be cleared away supposing the Captain and Executive Officer had both been killed by the explosion. The ship was sinking so rapidly it seemed impossible to get the launches cleared away, so I drove the men up the rigging to save themselves. After I got into the rigging I saw two of the boats had been cleared away and were picking up men who were overboard. As soon as I saw all were picked up, I sent one of the boats to the *Canandaigua* for assistance. Both boats left for the *Canandaigua* about the same time. The *Canandaigua* then came down to us and picked us off.

Question by the Court. What particular duty was assigned to you on board of the *Housatonic*?

Answer. Sailing Master's duty.

Question by the Court. What was the depth of water at the anchorage of the *Housatonic* at low water, and at about what stage of the tide did she sink?

Answer. There was about twenty-five feet at low water, and she sank at about half flood.

Question by the Court. What was the bearing and distance of Fort Sumter from the *Housatonic*, and what was the nearest land to her, and how far distant?

Answer. Fort Sumter bore W.N.W. 5⅖ miles distant. Long Island was the nearest land, about 2¼ miles distant.

Question by the Court. Describe particularly the apparent dimensions, shape and appearance of the object which you saw alongside.

Answer. It looked to be about 20 feet long and 2½ feet wide, and resembled a very old water logged piece of timber.

Question by the Court. Did you see it at any other time than the one stated?

Answer. At no other time.

Question by the Court. Did the explosion occur while it was alongside the ship?

Answer. It did.

Question by the Court. State the condition and preparation of the *Housatonic* as regards readiness for action on the night of the 17th inst.

Answer. The Battery was all cast loose; the Pivot-guns pivoted in Broadside; the watch armed,

and those who were not on lookout, or at the chain, were kept at their guns.

Question by the Court. State particularly all the effects of the explosion which came under your observation.

Answer. The explosion started me off my feet. And I saw fragments of the deck abaft the mizzen mast blown up into the air. The explosion was rather sharp, but not louder than a 12 pdr. Howitzer. I saw a very large quantity of black smoke, but no column of water, and no flame. She commenced sinking aft very rapidly, and by the time I got to the smoke stack, the water was up to my ankles there; she continued to sink until she was completely submerged, about three minutes after the explosion. When her fore foot was about six feet from the bottom, she keeled heavily to Port.

Question by the Court. What was the state of the weather force and direction of the wind on the night of the 17th at about the time the *Housatonic* sank?

Answer. The weather was fine, clear and bright moonlight; the sea was quite smooth; the wind was light and I think it was about N.N.W.

Question by the Court. Were order and discipline preserved on the *Housatonic*, and were the Officers and crew prompt in obeying orders from the time you got on deck until she sank?

Answer. Order and discipline were preserved until she commenced sinking, when many of the landsmen jumped overboard; the Officers and crew were prompt in obeying orders.

Question by the Court. Do you know of anything that was omitted to be done that could have been done to save the ship?

Answer. I do not.

Question by the Court. Where were the Captain and Executive Officer about the time of the explosion?

Answer. The Captain was on the horse block on the starboard quarter firing at the object alongside and the Executive Officer was standing alongside of him.

Question by the Court. Did you hear the Captain or Executive Officer give any orders after you got on deck? If yea, state them.

Answer. I heard the Captain give orders twice to slip the chain, which had already been done, though it had not run out of the hawser pipe.

Question by the Court. At what time did it run out?

Answer. As soon as she commenced backing; I heard it run out when I got about halfway aft on my return from seeing it had been unshackled.

The testimony having been read over to the witness and pronounced correct by him, he withdrew.

Acting Master's Mate Lewis A. Comthwait was then called and duly sworn according to law.

Question by Judge Advocate. Please state your name and rank in the service of the United States.

Answer. Lewis A. Comthwait, Acting Master's Mate.

Question by the Judge Advocate. What vessel have you been last attached to, and how long have you been so attached?

Answer. The U.S. Steam Sloop *Housatonic*; I joined her December 4th, 1863.

Question by Judge Advocate. State all you know in relation to the late disaster that befell the *Housatonic*.

Answer. I went on watch on the forecastle at 8 P.M. February 17th and about 8:45 P.M. the lookout on the starboard cathead reported something adrift on the water, about two points on the starboard bow, and about 100 yards distant. I then made it out with my glasses and it looked to me like a log with two lumps as large as XV inch shell bones on it, about ten feet apart. There was a break of the water forward and aft and between these two lumps. As soon as I saw it, I ran aft and reported it to the Officer of the Deck, who was on the bridge, and his glass turned in the direction of this object. I asked him if he saw it, and he replied, "Call all hands to Quarters." I then called the Quarter Gunner and told him to beat the gong. The order was then given to slip the chain. I saw forward, knocked the pin out of the shackle and reported the chain slipped, though at that time it had not run out. Immediately the inquiry was made from the quarter deck whether the chain was slipped. It began to run out of the hawse pipe and I ran aft to report it. When I got abreast the engine room hatch the explosion took place. There was then a general rush forward, and I ran with the crowd, crying out to clear away the boats. They succeeded in clearing away the gig and 3rd cutter, the rest being swamped, except the starboard launch, which could not be cleared. The ship then began to settle by the stern and lurched heavily to port by the time the water on deck had reached the smokestack. I was then in the fore rig-

ging, and all who were in it began to lay down from aloft to prevent her careening entirely over. She settled on the bottom in about three minutes from the time the explosion took place. The two boats that were cleared away then picked up the men who had jumped overboard. The gig then went to the *Canandaigua* for assistance.

Question by the Court. How long a time elapsed after the order was given to slip the cable before it was actually slipped?

Answer. About two minutes.

Question by the Court. Did you see the object in the water at any other time than you have stated?

Answer. I saw it as I was running forward after reporting it; it was abreast of the starboard forward pivot-gun's port, about 30 feet off.

Question by the Court. What was the direction in which it was moving?

Answer. It was moving astern, parallel to the ship's keel.

Question by the Court. Did it present the same appearance as when you first saw it?

Answer. It did, though the protuberances looked much larger than before.

Question by the Court. When you first discovered it, was it moving? If so, in what direction? Was its movement moderate or rapid?

Answer. It seemed to be moving and approaching the starboard bow, obliquely to the keel; it looked as though it was only drifting towards us.

Question by the Court. What time elapsed between your first discovering it and the explosion?

Answer. About four minutes.

Question by the Court. State particularly all the effects of the explosion which came under your notice.

Answer. I was standing on the port side, abreast the smokestack, facing aft, when the explosion took place. I heard no report, merely the crashing of the timbers, and saw pieces of the deck thrown into the air, as high as the mizzen top. There was a heavy black smoke, no flame and no column of water.

The testimony having been read over to the witness, and pronounced correct by him, he withdrew.

At 3 P.M. the Court adjourned to meet at 10 A.M. on Monday February 29th, or as soon thereafter as practicable.

12:10 P.M. Monday Feb. 29, 1864

The Court met pursuant to adjournment. Present –

Capt. Jos. F. Green
Capt. John De Camp
Comdr. J. C. Williamson
Lieut. Jas. B. Young, USMC Judge Advocate
The record of Saturday's proceedings was read over and approved. Lieut. F. J. Higginson was then called and duly sworn according to law.

Question by Judge Advocate. Please state your name and rank in the service of the United States.

Answer. F. J. Higginson. Lieutenant.

Question by Judge Advocate. What vessel have you been last attached to? How long have you been so attached and what special duty was assigned to you in that vessel.

Answer. The U. S. Steam Sloop *Housatonic*, since October 1863. I was executive officer.

Question by Judge Advocate. State all you know in reference to the late disaster that befell the *Housatonic*.

Answer. About 9 P.M. February 17th, I was in my room, when I heard the Officer of the Deck give the order to slip the chain. I went on deck immediately, found the Officer of the Deck on the bridge, and asked him the cause of the alarm; he pointed abaft the starboard beam on the water and said there it is. I then saw something resembling a plank moving towards the ship at the rate of 3 or 4 knots; it came close alongside, a little forward of the mizzen mast on the starboard side. It then stopped and appeared to move off slowly. I then went down from the bridge and took the rifle from the lookout on the horse block on the starboard quarter and fired it at this object. I then took the rifle from the lookout on the port quarter, returned to the starboard quarter, and attempted to fire at the object with this piece from the horse block, but it missed fire. I then laid it down on the horse block, stepped down on the deck, and immediately afterwards an explosion took place, throwing me down on the deck. When I got up I found the ship keeled over to port and sinking, the water being on a level with the deck in the after part of the ship. I then got with the port-quarter boat and attempted to clear away the stoppers; there were three or four men in the boat with me; before we could clear away the boat, she swamped, washing me out. I got hold of an oar in the water and commenced swimming towards the ship when I was picked up by the gig. I then took into the gig a number of men who were in the water and pulled towards the ship. Seeing that no alarm

had been given, I pulled towards the *Canandaigua* and informed them that the *Housatonic* was sunk. When I got up from being thrown on the deck I saw a column of smoke on the starboard side abreast of No. 7 gun port, forward of the mizzen mast.

Question by the Court. How far distant from the ship was the object when you first saw it, and in what direction was it moving?

Answer. About 80 yards distant, moving towards the ship at right angles to the keel, and nearly abreast of the mizzen mast.

Question by the Court. How far distant was it when you attempted to fire at it the second time, and was it moving?

Answer. About ten yards distant and it appeared to be stationary.

Question by the Court. Describe as accurately as possible the appearance of the object at the time referred to.

Answer. It had the appearance of a plank, sharp at both ends; it was entirely on a wash with the water, and there was a glimmer of light through the top of it, as though through a dead light. It appeared to be about 15 or 20 feet long, with about 5 feet beam. I did not notice any projections on it.

Question of the Court. What interval of time elapsed between your first seeing it and the explosion?

Answer. About three minutes.

Question of the Court. State particularly the preparation of the *Housatonic* for action, and the precautions observed on the night of the 17th inst. to discover the approach, and to repel an attack of the enemy.

Answer. The guns were cast loose, the Rifle on the forecastle pivoted on the port-bow: Gun No. 4 – 100 pdr. Rifle pivot—was pivoted on the starboard beam: gun No. 7 -- XI inch pivot -- pivoted on the port-beam. Broadside guns cast loose, with the luffs choked. The chain was ready for slipping and men stationed by it ready to slip if required. Lookouts were stationed, one on each cathead, gangway and quarter, armed with rifles. The remainder of the watch, armed as at quarters, on deck. A Quarter Gunner was stationed to beat the gong and fire rockets. The Officer of the Deck, officer of the forecastle, and Quartermaster were all supplied with night glasses. The engine was ready for backing; the order was they should have 25 lbs. of steam on during the night. The general orders to the Officer of the Deck, passed through me, were, that in case of discovering anything suspicious he was to slip the chain, beat to quarters, and back the engine as quickly as possible, at the same time informing the Captain. The order was given to back in order to prevent the slip rope from fouling the propeller.

Question by the Court. State the number and rank of officers comprising the watch on deck at and previous to the explosion.

Answer. There were two officers: an Acting Master in charge of the quarterdeck and an Acting Master's Mate on the forecastle.

Question by the Court. Did the ship have stern-board when the explosion occurred?

Answer. I do not know positively, but I think she did.

Question by the Court. State, if you know, at what time the cable was slipped and the propeller in motion.

Answer. About a minute after the Officer of the Deck gave the order the cable was slipped and the propeller was in motion about the same time.

Question by the Court. Could a gun or guns of the battery have been brought to bear on the object at anytime after its discovery? If nay, state the reason they were not.

Answer. No gun could have been brought to bear; none were fired, because none could be brought to bear.

At 12:15 P.M. the Court took a recess.

At 3 P.M. the Court re-assembled; all the members and the Judge Advocate present.

Lieut. Higginson was re-called and his examination continued.

Question by the Court. What was the state of the weather and sea, force and direction of the wind and tide, at about the time the *Housatonic* was blown up and sank? And what was the depth of water at her anchorage at low water?

Answer. The weather was clear and pleasant -- moonlight, not very bright; the sea was smooth; wind about N. W. force 2; it was about low water and there was about 28 feet of water at her anchorage at low water.

Question by the Court. What was the bearing and distance of Fort Sumter from, and what was the nearest land to, the *Housatonic* and how far distant?

Answer. Fort Sumter bore about W. N. W. six

miles distant. The battery on Breach Inlet, Sullivan's Island, was the nearest land, about 2½ miles distant.

Question by the Court. State particularly all the effects of the explosion that came under your observation.

Answer. The ship was shaken violently and caused to sink immediately, settling by the stern, keeling over to port as she sank. Many articles about the deck floated off and drifted astern when she sank. I heard a report, not very loud, a low stunning crash, a smothered sound.

Question by the Court. How long after the explosion occurred was the hull of the ship completely submerged?

Answer. About five or six minutes.

Question by the Court. Were order and discipline preserved on board the *Housatonic*, and were the officers and crew prompt obeying orders up to the time of her sinking?

Answer. Order and discipline were preserved; the officers and crew were prompt in obeying orders.

Question by the Court. Do you know anything that was omitted to be done that could have been done to save the ship? If yea, state it.

Answer. I do not.

Question by the Court. Did you see the Captain on deck during the alarm? If so, where was he, and what orders did he give?

Answer. He stood with me on the starboard horse block, and fired his gun at the object in the water. I heard him give no orders.

The testimony having been read over to the witness, and approved by him, he withdrew.

At 3:45 P.M. the Court adjourned to meet tomorrow, Tuesday morning at 10 o'clock, or as soon thereafter as practicable.

10:50 A.M. Tuesday, March 1, 1864

The Court met pursuant to adjournment. Present:

Capt. Jos. F. Green

Capt. Jno. DeCamp

Comdr. J. C. Williamson

Lieut. Jas. B. Young, Judge Advocate

The record of yesterday's proceedings was read over and approved.

2nd Asst. Engineer C. F. Mayer Jr. was then called and duly sworn according to law.

Question by Judge Advocate. Please state your

name and rank in the service of the United States.

Answer. C. F. Mayer, Jr., 2nd Assistant Engineer.

Question by Judge Advocate. What vessel have you been last attached to?

Answer. U. S. Steam Sloop *Housatonic*.

Question by Judge Advocate. What position did you hold on the *Housatonic* at the time of the late disaster?

Answer. I was senior Engineer.

Question by Judge Advocate. What were the general orders for the night in your department?

Answer. To keep 25 lbs. of steam, keep heavy banked fires, be ready to get under way at any time, and ready for backing.

Question by Judge Advocate. Were you in the engine room at the time the explosion occurred? If Yea, state the effects of it that came under your observation.

Answer. I was. Three bells were struck a few seconds after I got there, the engine was immediately backed, and had made three or four revolutions when I heard the explosion, accompanied by a sound of rushing water and crashing of timbers and metal. Immediately the engine went with great velocity as if the propeller had been broken off. I then throttled her down, but with little effect. I then jumped up the hatch, saw the ship was sinking and gave orders for all hands to go on deck.

Question by the Court. What amount of steam was there in the boiler, and were the fires heavily banked at about the time of the explosion?

Answer. About 26 lbs. of steam, and the fires were heavily banked.

Question by the Court. How many knots would 26 lbs. of steam propel the *Housatonic*?

Answer. With light winds and smooth sea the engine would have made 53 or 54 revolutions a minute, which would have propelled her for about 8½ knots. The steam might have fallen off, if we had got under way about 2 lbs. until the fires were spread which would have occupied about 5 minutes and then it would have risen.

Question by the Court. About how long after the order was given by the "Bell" to back was the engine in motion?

Answer. Almost immediately: only a few seconds.

Question by the Court. How long had the engine been in motion and how many revolutions was the engine making when the explosion occurred?

Answer. The engine had been in motion about six seconds and was making about thirty revolutions.

The testimony having been read over to the witness and pronounced correct by him he withdrew.

Robert F. Fleming, Landsman (colored) was then called and duly sworn according to law.

Question by Judge Advocate. What is your name, rate, and what ship have you been last on board of?

Answer. Robert F. Flemming, Landsman. U. S. Steam Sloop *Housatonic*.

Question by Judge Advocate. Where were you stationed at and previous to the explosion that sank the *Housatonic*?

Answer. I was on lookout on the starboard side of the forecastle.

Question by Judge Advocate. Did you see any object on the water approaching the ship just previous to the explosion? If Yea, state what you know about it.

Answer. I did. It was about 8:25 P.M. I saw something approaching the shipboard off the starboard bow, about two ship's lengths off, and reported it to the Officer of the forecastle. He told me it was a log. I then told him this was not floating with the tide as a log would, but moving across the tide. He still thought it was a log so I called the lookout from the Port side to see what it was. When the Officer of the forecastle saw this other lookout coming over he looked at the object through his glasses and then ran aft. I then cut away the ship buoy. By this time the object had got within about 30 feet of the starboard quarter. They then beat to quarters. I ran aft and before I got to my quarters, at No. 4 gun, the explosion took place. The ship began to settle by the stem immediately, and I ran forward again and when I got on the forecastle I saw the object about six or eight feet from the starboard quarter, apparently stationary, and I fixed my musket at it. I then went into the fore-top carrying my musket and accoutrements with me and afterwards taking them to the *Canandaigua* and stayed there until I was picked off by the *Canandaigua*'s boats.

Question by the Court. Describe particularly the appearance, shape and dimensions of the object you saw in the water.

Answer. It appeared to be about 22 feet long,

only each end visible, the water washing over amidships, each end about 22 inches out of water. I could not judge its width, as it was broadside on.

Question by the Court. How long a time elapsed from the time you first saw it until the explosion.

Answer. About six minutes.

Question by the Court. How long a time was it from the time you first reported it to the Officer of the forecastle until he ran aft?

Answer. About 1½ minutes, he left the forecastle, but did not get aft before they beat to Quarters.

Question by the Court. Did you see this object at any time after you fired at it?

Answer. I did not. When the *Canandaigua* got astern, and lying a thwart of the *Housatonic*, about four ships lengths off, while I was in the fore-rigging. I saw a blue light on the water just ahead of the *Canandaigua*, and on the starboard quarters of the *Housatonic*.

Question by the Court. Do you know who unshackled the cable? If so, state who.

Answer. I do not know.

Question by the Court. How long after you first discovered this object did they beat to quarters?

Answer. I am not positive, but I think about three minutes.

Question by the Court. Was the cable slipped at that time?

Answer. I do not know.

Question by the Court. Describe the effects of the explosion that came under your observation.

Answer. I was a little abaft the main mast on the Port side when the explosion took place. I heard a noise like a splash of wood in the water, I saw fragments of timber in the air.

Question by the Court. Did the ship have sternboard when the explosion took place?

Answer. I do not know.

The testimony having been read to the witness and pronounced correct by him, he withdrew.

At 1:25 P.M. the Court took a recess.

At 2:05 P.M. the Court reassembled all the members and the Judge Advocate present.

Third Assistant Engineer J. W. Holickan was then called and duly sworn according to law.

Question by Judge Advocate. State your name, rank in the service of the United States, and what vessel have you been last attached to?

Answer. James W. Holickan, Third Assistant Engineer, U. S. Steam Sloop *Housatonic*.

Question by Judge Advocate. Were you on watch on the night of February 17th? if so, at what time and state what were your orders with regard to the readiness of the Engine for service. Were these orders carried out fully on the night in question?

Answer. I took charge of the watch in the engine room at 8 P.M.; the standing orders were to keep heavy banked fires and 25 lbs. of steam from 6 P.M. until 6 a.m.; to keep everything ready for getting underway at a moment's warning, and to have the engine ready for backing. The orders were fully carried out on that night; to the best of my knowledge there was a little over 25 lbs. of steam on as we endeavored always to be rather over than under the mark; the fires were heavily banked and in good order.

Question by Judge Advocate. Were you in the engine room at and previous to the time the explosion occurred? If Yea, state all that was done there.

Answer. I was. I heard the gong beat for Quarters, and gave orders to have everything ready for starting the engine. Immediately three bells were struck and I gave orders to open the stop valves and back the engine. The engine had made about ten or twelve revolutions, at the rate of about thirty per minute, before I heard the crashing of timber.

Question by Judge Advocate. State all of the effects of the explosion that came under your observation.

Answer. I was standing by the throttle valve and was staggered by the shock and the engine commenced turning so rapidly I closed the throttle valve, supposing some part of the machinery had given way, but it seemed to have no effect.

Question by the Court. Under all the circumstances the *Housatonic* was then placed in, at anchor, at what speed would 25 lbs. of steam have driven her, had she got underway?

Answer. We could have made about 52 revolutions per minute, which would have driven her about 7½ knots at the start, and we could have increased it gradually to 8½ knots.

Question by the Court. What time elapsed after the order was given to back the engine before it was actually in motion?

Answer. About fifteen or twenty seconds.

The testimony having been read over to the witness and pronounced correct by him, he withdrew.

This painting by Herb Mott depicts the *Hunley* bearing down on the *Housatonic*. The submarine is shown with its spar torpedo attached to the upper part of its bow, a common depiction. However, studies of the partially buried wreck suggest that the spar may have been attached to the lower part of the bow.

At 2:35 P.M. the Court adjourned to meet at 10 o'clock tomorrow, Wednesday morning, or as soon thereafter as practicable.

11:45 A.M. Wednesday, March 2, 1864.

The Court met pursuant to adjournment. Present:

Capt. Jos. F. Green

Capt. Jno. DeCamp

Comdr. J. C. Williamson

Lieut. Jas. B. Young, Judge Advocate

The record of yesterday's proceedings was read over and approved.

Acting Ensign F. H. Crandall was then called and duly sworn according to law.

Question by Judge Advocate. State your name, rank in the service of the United States, and what vessel you have been last attached to.

Answer. F. H. Crandall, Acting Ensign, U.S. Steam Sloop *Housatonic*.

Question by Judge Advocate. State all that came under your observation in relation to the loss of the *Housatonic* on the night of February 17th, between the first alarm and the explosion.

Answer. I was sitting in the Paymaster's room about 9 P.M. when I heard the Officer of the Deck call out "All hands to Quarters," at the same time the gong was sounded. I immediately rushed on deck, thinking a blockade runner had been sighted or the Rebel Rams had come out. Having charge of the Powder Division I then went into the cabin and took the magazine and shell room keys from the Captain's sleeping room. Just as I was coming up the stairway of the Cabin I heard someone call out "Shoot at the boat, it is a Torpedo going to blow us up." I observed the men on deck were firing at something directly alongside, and had just time to get to the Starboard after pivot-gun's port and to catch a glimpse of the torpedo boat, which was about five or six feet off, when the explosion occurred.

Question by the Court. What interval of time elapsed between the first alarm that you heard and the explosion?

Answer. About three minutes.

Question by the Court. Was the magazine opened, or was any attempt made to open it other than stated?

Answer. It was not open and I do not know of any other attempt being made. I retained the keys of the magazine and shell room.

The testimony having been read over to the witness and pronounced correct by him, he withdrew.

C. P. Slade, Landsman (colored) was then called and duly sworn according to law.

Question by Judge Advocate. State your name, rate, and what vessel you have been last on board of.

Answer. C. P. Slade, Landsman, U.S. Steam Sloop *Housatonic*.

Question by Judge Advocate. Where were you stationed at and previous to the explosion that sank the *Housatonic*?

Answer. On lookout on the Port cathead.

Question by Judge Advocate. Did you see anything unusual on the water about that time? If so, state all you know on the subject.

Answer. The lookout on the Starboard cathead called me over and said there was a Torpedo coming. I went over and looked at it; it was about one and a half ship's lengths off the starboard beam, moving rather fast, towards the after pivot gun's post, it looked like an old log about 24 feet long, only the two ends visible, the middle being underwater. The Master Mate was on the top gallant forecastle at the time talking to the Captain of the forecastle. I did not hear what about. About three minutes after I went over to the starboard side, he went aft and soon after they beat to Quarters. I then started aft and fired at it out of the starboard Port of the pivot gun between the fore and main masts, it being then about ten yards from the starboard quarter, and moving towards the ship's side. I went towards my Quarters at the after pivot gun, and when I got by the steerage hatch the explosion occurred.

Question by Judge Advocate. Did you see this object at any other time than stated? If so, state all about it.

Answer. I did not.

Question by Judge Advocate. Did you report seeing this object to the Officer of the Forecastle?

Answer. I did not.

Question by the Court. What time elapsed between your first seeing it and the explosion?

Answer. About fifteen minutes.

Question by the Court. What time from your first seeing it to the beat to quarters?

Answer. About five minutes.

Question by the Court. About the time of the discovery of this object did you hear the conversation between the lookout on the starboard cathead and the Officer of the Forecastle? If so, state it.

Answer. I did not.

Question by the Court. How long after they beat to Quarters did the explosion occur?

Answer. About two minutes.

The testimony having been read over to the witness, and pronounced correct by him, he withdrew.

George W. Kelly, Cooper, was then called, and duly sworn according to law.

Question by Judge Advocate. State your name, rate, and the vessel you have been last on board of.

Answer. George W. Kelly, Cooper, U.S. Steam Sloop *Housatonic*.

Question by Judge Advocate. Did you see any object on the water, previous to the explosion that sank the *Housatonic*? If so, state all you know about it.

Answer. I was on the Forecastle a few minutes before 9 P.M. February 17th. I saw something on the water looking like a capsized boat, about 25 feet long, about three points on the starboard bow, about 75 yards distant, moving astern nearly parallel with the keel. Before I went on the Forecastle, I heard the lookout on the starboard cathead say he saw a droll looking log moving across the tide; afterwards I heard him say "if no one is going to report this, I will cut the buoy adrift myself and get ready for slipping." His remarks were what attracted my attention. I was on the Forecastle only a few seconds then went aft to my Quarters at the after pivot guns; when I got to the forward end of this gun's starboard port I saw this object again about fifteen yards from the ship making a sort of circle towards the starboard quarter. I then started forward to get my primer box, it was not my watch on deck, and when I got abreast the engine room hatch the explosion occurred. I do not think it was over half a minute from the time I first saw this object until the explosion occurred.

Question by the Court. How long after you first saw this object did they beat to Quarters?

Answer. About half a minute.

The testimony having been read over to the witness and pronounced correct by him, he withdrew.

H. S. Gifford, Coxswain, was then called and duly sworn according to law.

Question by Judge Advocate. State your name, rate, and the vessel you have been last on board of.

Answer. Henry S. Gifford, Coxswain, and acting 2nd Captain of the Forecastle, U. S. Steam Sloop *Housatonic*.

Question by Judge Advocate. Did you see any strange object on the water previous to the explosion that sank the *Housatonic*? if so, state all you know about it.

Answer. I was on the Forecastle, it being my watch on deck, talking with the Officer of the Forecastle about 8:45 P.M., when the lookout on the starboard cathead asked "what is that coming?"; the Officer of the Forecastle then looked at it through his glasses, said it looked like a log, and then started aft. The lookout then said it was a queer looking log, and asked if he had better fire at it. I told him, Yes, as I had orders to fire at anything I might see on the water. He snapped his gun at it. I then left him, went down on deck, and got as far as the Pivot gun between the fore and main masts, when I looked out of the starboard port and saw this object about 30 or 40 yards from the ship, rounding to towards the starboard quarters. Just then I heard Mr. Crosby give orders to beat the gong, slip the chain and ring three bells; these orders were all obeyed immediately. I then went to my Quarters at No. 6 gun, and in about a minute the explosion occurred. Just before the explosion I heard Mr. Crosby tell the men around they had better go forward as it was a Torpedo and they would all be blown up; the words were hardly out of his mouth before the ship was blown up.

Question by Judge Advocate. Did you see this object when you were on the Forecastle? if so, how far distant was it from the ship and how was it moving?

Answer. I saw it about a point forward of the starboard cathead, about 75 yards distant; it was approaching the starboard quarter obliquely at the rate of about 2½ knots. After it got abeam it seemed to be moving faster, but in the same direction.

Question by Judge Advocate. Describe its appearance, shape and dimensions.

Answer. It looked to be about 25 or 30 feet long, sharp at both ends, with two protuberances about the size of mess kettles, each ten feet from the end. Amidships it looked to be six inches out of water and at the ends about a foot. I saw no smoke indicating steam to propel it; but there was white water surrounding it.

Question by the Court. What time elapsed between your first seeing it and the explosion?

Answer. About five minutes.

Question by the Court. What time elapsed between the lookout's calling your attention to this object and the Officer of the Forecastle's going aft?

Answer. Not more than a minute.

Question by the Court. Had the lookout called the Officer of the Forecastle's attention to it before the time referred to in the preceding question?

Answer. He had not.

Question by the Court. Do you know of anything that was omitted to be done, that could have been done to save the ship?

Answer. I do not.

The testimony having been read over to the witness, and pronounced correct by him, he withdrew.

At 2:55 P.M. the Court adjourned to meet at 10 o'clock tomorrow, Thursday morning, or as soon thereafter as practicable.

11:15 A.M. Friday, March 4, 1864.

The Court met pursuant to adjournment, being unable to meet yesterday on account of the roughness of the sea and strength of the wind. Present.

Capt. Jos. F. Green

Capt. John DeCamp

Comdr. J. C. Williamson

Lieut. Jos. B. Young, Judge Advocate

The record of Wednesday's proceedings was read over and approved.

James Timmons, Quarter Master, was then called and duly sworn according to law.

Question by Judge Advocate. State your name, rate, and what vessel you have been last attached to.

Answer. James Timmons, Quarter Master, U.S. Steam Sloop *Housatonic*.

Question by Judge Advocate. Were you on watch the night of February 17th? if so, at what time, and when did you keep it?

Answer. I went on watch at 8 P.M. on the Quarter Deck.

Question by Judge Advocate. Did you see any strange object on the water previous to the explosion that sank the *Housatonic*? If so, state all you know about it.

Answer. About 8:40 P.M. I was on the Port side looking seaward, when I heard the Officer of the Deck call out "What is this on the water?" I ran over to the starboard side and saw a white ripple on the water a little forward of the beam about 100

yards distant, heading about for the gangway, moving towards the ship at right angles to the keel. Then the Officer of the Deck called out, "Beat to Quarters, call the Captain, and slip the chain." When the gong beat, this object looked like a log, and gave a slew towards the starboard Quarter of the ship, which made me think it was something more than a log. I ran forward nearly to the foremast, and repeated the order to slip the chain. I then ran aft and heard the Captain give orders to slip the chain, and back her. I then ran to the bell, but before I got there the Engineer had struck three bells. I then went aft and found them firing musketry over the starboard quarters at something close alongside. I then went and took the musket from the lookout on the Port gangway, ran aft and by the time I got to the Wardroom hatch the explosion occurred.

Question by the Court. How long a time elapsed from your first seeing it until the explosion?

Answer. About four minutes.

Question by the Court. Were the orders to beat to Quarters and slip the chain promptly obeyed, and was anything to your knowledge omitted to be done that could have been done to save the ship?

Answer. The orders were promptly obeyed. Nothing to my knowledge was omitted that could have been done to save the ship.

The testimony having been read over to the witness, and pronounced correct by him, he withdrew.

Thos. H. Kelly, Seaman, was then called and duly sworn according to law.

Question by Judge Advocate. State your name, rate, and whether you were attached to U.S. Steam Sloop *Housatonic* on February 17th.

Answer. Thomas H. Kelly, Seaman, doing duty as Quarter Gunner. I was attached to the *Housatonic*.

Question by Judge Advocate. Were you on watch on deck just previous to the explosion that sank the *Housatonic*? If so, state all you know about it.

Answer. I was on watch, and was stationed with a slow match to fire the rockets, and to beat the Gong for Quarters. About 8:45 P.M. I was by the after pivot gun when I heard the lookout on the starboard cathead report seeing something like a log coming towards the ship. Mr. Comthwait replied it was nothing but a log. About ten minutes afterwards I heard Mr. Crosby ask the Quarter Master what was that coming. I then went directly to the starboard port of the after pivot gun, looked over the side, and saw an object in the water, about 30 feet long with a hub on each end as large as a mess kettle, about 10 yards distant, right abreast of this port and moving towards the mizzen rigging. I sang out "That's a Torpedo," and Mr. Crosby told me to beat to Quarters, and gave orders to slip the chain. It then seemed to stop. I beat to Quarters, came aft, looked out of the same Port and the explosion occurred.

Question by Judge Advocate. How long a time elapsed between your first seeing it, and the explosion?

Answer. About fifteen minutes.

Question by the Court. How long after the discovery of the object in the water by the lookout at the cathead, did you beat the gong for quarters?

Answer. About ten minutes.

Question by the Court. At what speed was this object approaching the vessel when you saw it?

Answer. About four knots.

Question by the Court. When you heard the lookout at the cathead report the object in the water, to whom did he report it, and what were the words of his report?

Answer. To Mr. Comthwait, Officer of the Forecastle, he said, "There is something coming that looks like a log: it looks very suspicious."

Question by the Court. Where was Mr. Comthwait at the time the report was made to him, and was the report made to him in a moderate or loud tone of voice?

Answer. He was on the Forecastle; the report was made in a loud tone.

Question by the Court. How near to the after pivot gun were you when you heard the report made to Mr. Comthwait?

Answer. About 15 feet forward of it—I was abaft the main mast.

Question by the Court. You have stated you were near the after pivot gun at the time this report was made to Mr. Comthwait; how then do you know that the lookout at the cathead made this report, and that it was made to Mr. Comthwait?

Answer. I heard the lookout call Mr. Comthwait's name and I saw him on the Forecastle.

Question by the Court. Were the orders to slip the chain and beat to Quarters promptly obeyed? And do you know of anything that was omitted to

be done that could have been done to save the ship?

Answer. The orders were promptly obeyed. If the object had been reported when it was first discovered No. 4 gun—100 pdr. Pivot gun between the five and main rigging—might have been trained on it. I know of nothing else that could have been done to save the ship.

Question by the Court. You have stated in your evidence that you first saw the suspicious object from the after pivot port, about ten yards from the ship; how then do you know that No. 4 gun could have been trained on it when it was first discovered?

Answer. When I saw it from the after port it was coming from a direction that made me suppose No. 4 gun could have been trained, when it was first discovered.

Question by the Court. On the night of the 17th, tell which side was No. 4 gun pivoted?

Answer. Starboard side.

The testimony having been read over to the witness and pronounced correct by him, he withdrew.

John Saunders, Landsman, colored, was then called and duly sworn according to law.

Question by Judge Advocate. State your name, and rate.

Answer. John Saunders, Landsman.

Question by Judge Advocate. Were you on board the *Housatonic* on the night of February 17th? if so, where were you stationed previous to the explosion?

Answer. I was. I was stationed on lookout on the Starboard Quarter.

Question by Judge Advocate. Did you see anything strange on the water? If so, state all you know about it.

Answer. About 8:45 P.M. I heard the Officer of the Deck say something was coming to blow us up. I looked and saw something forward of the beam, about 40 or 50 yards off, looking like a log, even with the water, with a knob about a foot high on it, moving towards the mizzen chains, quite fast. I tried to fire my musket at it, but it snapped twice. The First Lieutenant then came, took the piece from me, and fired at it. The object was then right under the ship. The First Lieutenant then got down, and the Captain got up. I got down on deck, went over to the Port side, and to the wheel to take the hood off and then I do not remember anything until I found myself under where the wheel was.

Question by Judge Advocate. How long was it from the time you first saw this object until you went to take the hood off the wheel?

Answer. I can not tell anything of the time.

Question by the Court. How long was it from the time you first saw this object until the Captain got up on the Quarter?

Answer. I do not know. It was a short time.

The testimony having been read over to the witness, and pronounced correct by him, he withdrew.

Assistant Paymaster John S. Woolson was then called and duly sworn according to law.

Question by Judge Advocate. Please state your name, rank in the service of the United States, and what vessel you have been last attached to.

Answer. John S. Woolson—Assistant Paymaster—U. S. Steam Sloop *Housatonic*.

Question by Judge Advocate. Please state how many of the Officers and crew of the *Housatonic* have been missing since the late disaster; with their names and rank.

Answer. Two Officers are missing, Ensign E. L. Hasiltine, and Captain's Clerk Charles O. Muzzey. And three men: John Williams, Quarter Master, Theodore Parker, Landsman, Colored, and John Walsh, 2nd Class Fireman. I have made as careful an examination as I could in the absence of my Master Roll.

The testimony having been read over to the witness, and pronounced correct by him, he withdrew.

John Desmond, Boatswain's Mate, was then called and duly sworn according to law.

Question by Judge Advocate. State your name, rate, and the vessel you were attached to February 17th.

Answer. John Desmond—Botswain's Mate—U.S. Steam Sloop *Housatonic*.

Question by Judge Advocate. Were you on watch at the time the explosion occurred that sank the *Housatonic*? if so, state all you know about it.

Answer. I was. The first I knew of any alarm was the gong beating to Quarters. I then went to my Gun—Broadside 32 pdr. in the starboard gangway and trained it on the Quarter by orders of the Officer of the Division, but saw nothing myself. The explosion occurred, and the ship settled so much in the water I was forced to leave the gun.

Question by the Court. Do you know of any-

thing that was omitted to be done that could have been done to save the ship from the time you went to your Quarters until the ship sank?

Answer. Nothing.

The testimony having been read over to the witness, and pronounced correct by him, he withdrew.

At 2:30 P.M. the Court adjourned to meet tomorrow, Saturday morning at 10 o'clock or as soon thereafter as practicable, on board the U. S. Steam Sloop *Canandaigua* for the purpose of taking the evidence of Captain Pickering, who is unable to leave the *Canandaigua*.

U. S. Steam Sloop *Canandaigua*

11 A.M. Saturday, March 5, 1864.

The Court met pursuant to adjournment. Present:

Capt. Jos. F. Green

Capt. John DeCamp

Comdr. J. C. Williamson

Lieut. Jas. B. Young, Judge Advocate

The record of yesterday's proceedings was read over and approved.

Captain C. W. Pickering was then called and duly sworn according to law.

Question by Judge Advocate. State your name, rank, and the vessel you have last commanded.

Answer. Charles W. Pickering, Captain U. S. Navy late in command of the *Housatonic*.

Question by Judge Advocate. Please state all that came under your observation in relation to the late disaster that befell the *Housatonic*.

Answer. On February 17th a few minutes before 9 P.M.—the ship at anchor about 6 miles E.S.E. by Compass from Fort Sumter, riding at 75 fathoms starboard chain, heading about N.W. by W., wind from Northward and Westward nearly ahead—while seated at the cabin table overhauling a book of charts, I heard a confused sound and stir of excitement on deck. I heard the Officer of the Deck call the Orderly for the transmission of some information. I sprang from the table under the impression that a blockade runner was about. In snatching my cap I found I had taken Dr. Plant's by mistake, who was seated at the table with me at the time. I turned back, got my own, met the orderly at the cabin door, and passed him without waiting to receive his report. On reaching the deck I gave the order to slip and heard for the first time it was a torpedo, I think from the Officer of the Deck. I repeated the order to slip, and gave the order to go astern, and to open fire. I turned instantly, took my double barreled gun, loaded with buckshot, from Mr. Muzzey, my aid and clerk and jumped up on the horse block on the starboard Quarter, which the First Lieutenant had just left having fired a musket at the Torpedo. I hastily examined the Torpedo: it was shaped like a large whale boat, about two feet, more or less, under water; its position was at right angles to the ship, bows on, and the bows within two or three feet of the ship's side, about abreast of the mizzen mast, and I supposed it was then finding the torpedo on. I saw two projections or knobs about one third of the way from the bows. I fired at these, jumped down from the horse block, and ran up the port side of the Quarter Deck, as far as the mizzen mast, saying out "Go astern faster." The men were then huddling forward, I would not call them aft to the guns, as they could not be trained until the ship had got some distance from the Torpedo, and they were in a safer place. I thought of going forward myself to get clear of the Torpedo, but reflecting that my proper station was aft, I remained there, and was blown into the air the next instant from where I stood on the Port side abreast of the mizzen mast. I found myself in the water about where I stood previous to the explosion amongst broken timbers, the debris of panel work and planking. I succeeded in getting into the mizzen rigging very much bruised, and was rescued by a boat. The ship was then lying over on her Port side, so as to bring her Port Quarters boat under water she was raised forward and her fore rigging full of men. The interval of time between the explosion and my getting into the rigging is unknown to me.

Question by the Court. What was the interval of time between your firing at the Torpedo and the explosion?

Answer. About a minute; certainly not more than a minute and a half.

Question by the Court. What were the General Orders given to the Executive Officer and Officer of the Deck, and what was the state of preparation of the *Housatonic*, at night to discover and repel an attack of an enemy?

Answer. The orders to the Executive Officer and Officer of the Deck were to be for vigilant lookout, glasses in constant use—there were three glasses in use, by the Officer of the Deck, Officer of the Forecastle and Quarter Master, and six lookouts besides—and the moment he saw anything suspicious to slip the chain, sound the gong, without waiting for orders, and send for me to keep the engines reversed ready for going astern, as I had on a previous occasion got my slip rope foul of the propeller by going ahead. I had the Pivot guns pivoted in broadside, the 100 pdr. on the starboard side, and the XI inch on the Port side; the Battery all cast loose and loaded, and a round of cartridges kept in the arms chest so that two Broadsides could be fired before the reception of powder from the magazine. Two shell, two canister and two grape were kept by each gun. The Quarter Gunner was stationed by the match, with the gong. Watch and lookouts armed as at Quarters. Three rockets were kept in three stands ready for the necessary signal. Two men were stationed at the slip rope, and others at the chain stopper and shackle on the spar deck. The chain was prepared for slipping by reversing the shackle, bow aft instead of forward. The pin which confined the bolt removed and a wooden pen substituted and the shackle placed upon chain shoes fair for knocking the bolt out; so that all that was necessary to slip the chain was to strike the bolt with the sledge once, which broke the wooden pin, and drive the bolt across the deck, leaving the forward end of the chain clear of the shackle. I had all the necessary signals at hand, ready for an emergency. The order was to keep up 25 lbs. of steam at night always, and have everything ready for going astern instantly.

Question by the Court. What was the depth of water at low water at the *Housatonic*'s anchorage, and what was the state of the weather, and stage of the tide at the time of the explosion?

Answer. 26 or 27 feet at low water, it was a pleasant, moonlight night, with a fresh breeze and very cold, about half ebb tide, and 28 or 29 feet of water.

Question by the Court. Were all of your general and special orders observed that night? And was anything to your knowledge omitted to be done that could have been done to save the ship?

Answer. They were promptly obeyed. Nothing was omitted that could have been done. If I had had two minutes to work in, I could probably have saved the ship and sunk the Torpedo craft.

Question by the Court. Did you see the Torpedo craft at any other time than that you have stated?

Answer. I did not, although I looked in every direction about the ship from the mizzen rigging after the ship sank.

The testimony having been read over to the witness, and pronounced correct by him, he withdrew.

Assistant Surgeon William T. Plant was then called and duly sworn according to law.

Question by Judge Advocate. Please state your name, rank in the service of the United States, and what vessel you have been last attached to.

Answer. William T. Plant, Assistant Surgeon U. S. Navy, USS *Housatonic*.

Question by Judge Advocate. Have you taken any steps towards ascertaining the number of casualties that occurred on the night of February 17th, among the Officers and crew of the *Housatonic*? If so, please state all you know on the subject.

Answer. I have. The number lost, I believe to have been five, two officers Ensign E. C. Haseltine and Captain's Clerk C. O. Muzzey and three men. John Williams, Quarter Master; Theodore Parker, Landsman, colored, and Walsh, Fireman. There were two injured. Captain C. W. Pickering, and John Gough, Captain's steward, both painfully but not dangerously injured.

The testimony having been read over to the witness, and pronounced correct by him, he withdrew.

At 1:10 P.M. the Court adjourned to meet at 10 o'clock, Monday morning, March 7th, or as soon thereafter as practicable on board the U. S. Steam Frigate *Wabash*.

U. S. Steam Frigate *Wabash*.
10:50 A.M. Monday, March 7, 1864.
The Court met pursuant to adjournment. Present:
Capt. Jos. F. Green
Capt. John DeCamp
Comdr. J. C. Williamson
Lieut. Jas. B. Young, Judge Advocate
The record of Saturday's proceedings was read over and approved.

The testimony having been closed the Court was cleared for deliberation, and after maturely considering the evidence adduced find the following facts established:

First. That the U. S. Steamer *Housatonic* was blown up and sunk by a Rebel torpedo craft on the night of February 17th, Last at about 9 o'clock P.M., while lying at an anchor in 24 feet of water off Charleston S. C. bearing E. S. E. and distant from Fort Sumter about 5½ miles. The weather at the time of the occurrence was clear, the night bright

and moonlight, wind moderate from the Northward and Westward sea smooth and tide half ebb, the ship's head about W. N. W.

Second. That between 8:45 and 9 o'clock P.M. on said night an object in the water was discovered almost simultaneously by the Officer of the Deck and the lookout stationed at the Starboard cathead, on the starboard bow of the ship about 75 or 100 yards distant, having the appearance of a log. That on further and closer observation it presented a suspicious appearance, moved apparently with a speed of 3 or 4 knots in the direction of the Starboard Quarter of the ship, exhibiting two protuberances above, and making a slight ripple in the water.

Third. That the strange object approached the ship with a rapidity precluding a gun of the battery being brought to bear upon it, and finally came in contact with the ship on her starboard Quarter.

Fourth. That about one and a half minutes after the first discovery of the strange object the crew were called to Quarters, the cable slipped, and the engine backed.

Fifth. That an explosion occurred about three minutes after the first discovery of the object which blew up the after part of the ship, causing her to sink immediately after to the bottom, with her spar deck submerged.

Sixth. That several shots from small arms were fired at the object while it was alongside or near the ship before the explosion occurred.

Seventh. That the watch on deck, ship and ship's Battery were in all respects prepared for a sudden offensive or defensive movement. That lookouts were properly stationed, and vigilance observed and that Officers and crew promptly assembled at their Quarters.

Eighth. That order was preserved on board and orders promptly obeyed by Officers and crew up to the time of the sinking of the ship.

In view of the above facts the Court have to express the opinion that no further military proceedings are necessary.
J. F. Green
Captain & President
Jas. B. Young
2.Lieut. U. S. Marines
Judge Advocate
At 2:45 P.M. the Court adjourned sine die.
J. F. Green
Captain & President

Appendix B

THE *H. L. HUNLEY* ARCHAEOLOGY MANAGEMENT PLAN

Prepared by the South Carolina Institute of Archaeology and Anthropology (SCIAA) Hunley Project Working Group

Introduction

This is an update of the September 12, 1995 proposal for the management of the remains of the Confederate submarine *H. L. Hunley*. It was originally developed by the South Carolina Institute of Archaeology and Anthropology–Hunley Project Working Group (SCIAA–HPWG) at the request of the South Carolina Hunley Commission (a state commission authorized by the South Carolina State Legislature to oversee the state's interests in the *H. L. Hunley* by Concurrent Resolution S844 and H858 and pending bills S1014 and H4448). This proposal's purpose was, and continues to be, to provide the state Commission with technical data regarding appropriate methods for verification, assessment, and, as a result of that assessment, various scenarios regarding the vessel's future. Some additional background is necessary for understanding the changes that have been made in this proposal.

The South Carolina Institute of Archaeology and Anthropology is mandated to perform dual roles in research and management in archaeology on behalf of the state (SCCL 6013210). This mandate is further strengthened by a separate state law naming SCIAA as the manager all underwater antiquities located on the state's submerged lands (SCCL 547610 et seq.).

Unsurprisingly, this dual role often leads to confusion, both inside and outside the Institute, as to the proper role SCIAA must take for any given project. The *Hunley* project is a case in point. Initially, the NUMA–SCIAA search for the *Hunley* was conceived as a research effort. Once NUMA had announced it had discovered the *Hunley* (see below)

it became clear to SCIAA that its management role was paramount and it moved into that role. However, in the excitement of the *Hunley*'s discovery, and its immediate impact on the world, this change was often misunderstood in various press announcements.

With the announcement of the discovery of the *Hunley*, and the formation of a state Commission to oversee its future, the SCIAA formed the Hunley Project Working Group, seeing its role as directing state sponsored field work to assess the condition of the *H. L. Hunley* both archaeologically and in terms of conservation. Any future archaeological investigation by SCIAA–HPWG would be at the discretion and direction of the state Commission. Regardless of the SCIAA–HPWG future role in the possible raising, and conservation, of the *Hunley*, the Commission requested SCIAA to provide them with a number of scenarios concerning the *Hunley*'s future, and the result was SCIAA–HPWG's proposal dated September 12, 1995.

Since that time, the project has greatly evolved as the SC Hunley Commission and the Navy continue to negotiate title and a programmatic agreement. The following proposal has been revised to reflect this evolution in fulfillment of the SC Hunley Commission's charge to SCIAA–HPWG. No doubt, despite the planning presented herein, the project will continue to evolve, and readers are encouraged to keep tuning in to our updates.

Project History and Discovery

During the months of August and September 1994, the Underwater Archaeology Division of the South Carolina Institute of Archaeology and Anthropology (SCIAA) and Mr. Clive Cussler's National Underwater Marine Agency (NUMA) conducted a joint operation to locate the *H. L. Hunley*.

Progress was made in identifying a series of anomalies within the search area near the scattered remains of *USS Housatonic*. Mr. Cussler's team continued field operations and announced on May 9, 1995, that they had located the hull of the illfated submarine off Sullivan's Island, Charleston County, South Carolina. The coordinates for the find were given to the Naval Historical Center by NUMA later in 1995.

SCIAA's Hunley Project Working Group in keeping with its management role needs to verify the NUMA location and assess the condition of the *H. L. Hunley*. This will provide the base data for the accurate production and review of a Scope of Work and eventually a Request for Proposal that is expected to be made collaboratively with the appropriate state and federal agencies.

Site Protection

Protection of the wreck site has been a long standing concern of the SCIAA–HPWG and the SC Hunley Commission. It is essential that the appropriate law enforcement agencies continue to render surveillance and protection of the wreck site until such time as the vessel is recovered. Fortunately, the area in which the vessel is located continues to be under the protective surveillance of the United States Coast Guard. This surveillance has been extended indefinitely. Failing full recovery, the vessel's remains will need protection in perpetuity where it lies on the ocean floor. This is a direct result of the bounties placed on fragments of the vessel by relic and antiquities collectors. The Coast Guard deserves a great deal of thanks for their immediate response when approached by the state for assistance. Nonetheless, additional assistance from other federal and state agencies should be sought and coordinated with the Coast Guard to more equitably share the burden of protection.

Archaeology and Survey

In the interest of acquiring the base information with a minimum of disturbance to the vessel, tests have been conducted using newly available subbottom profiling equipment on other known wreck sites with good results. It is expected that formal identification, verification and assessment of the *H. L. Hunley* will be accomplished after the negotiations between the state and Navy are concluded. This has been planned at the technical level as a joint state and federal operation, but may be modified through agreement of the political entities overseeing this project. After this phase, the SCIAA will continue its legally mandated management functions with advice from two national scientific organizations, the Advisory Council on Underwater Archaeology (ACUA) and the American Institute for Conservation of Artistic and Historic Works (AIC), and the State Historic Preservation Office. Review and technical information derived from these interactions will be passed on to the SC Hunley Commission.

Identification and Verification of the Vessel

NUMA has reported that the *H. L. Hunley* site was embedded in at least three feet of sediment at the time it was located. The general area is extremely dynamic with well documented fluvial and sedimentary processes. It is unclear to what extent the exploratory dredging around the submarine may have loosened compacted substrates. It is possible that a typical sedimentary scouring and accumulation geomorphologic pattern has been created, which may enhance exposure, or covering, of the site during certain tidal conditions.

If the submarine is exposed, presenting a profile on the seabed, the site can be reacquired and initially recorded using side scan sonar. This technique relies on acoustic coneshaped beams that pass through the water column to the wreck and bounce back creating an image or outline of the object. The denser the material, and more integrity the object has, the stronger the signal. If the *H. L. Hunley* is still in the condition reported by the NUMA dive team, it should yield a sharp and diagnostic sonar image.

The present technical plan is for all sonar targets to be assessed jointly by the SCIAA and federal dive teams that are expected to be involved. Diving conditions in the survey area are generally poor with an average visibility of one to two feet and strong currents. This will require careful planning and coordination to maximize the information that can be recovered by the teams. The divers will take photographs, video footage and general measurements of the wreck site, with particular attention allocated to identifying external features for comparative data with the previous NUMA report and video.

If the target is covered with no exposed structures it will be assessed using a new generation of subbottom profiler. The subbottom profiler relies upon a narrowbeam acoustic signal that penetrates the seabed and substrate recording the outline and density of the target. These readings will provide a nonintrusive estimation and quantification of surviving structures of the vessel. Additionally, this instrument will display detailed data on the sedimentary composition in the vicinity of the target essential for accurately interpreting the site formation processes. A compilation of this type of information is critical for the production of the management plan.

The SCIAA's research vessels are adequate for the standard field work normally performed, but are inadequate as platforms for the specialized equipment necessary for this project. Conducting a marine survey to the professional standards required on this project calls for a vessel that meets three requirements. First, it must be a stable platform for the survey equipment. Second, it must be a platform that can protect the sensitive equipment from the elements and the effects of the sea. And finally, it must be a platform that has a precise navigation system that can be interfaced with the survey equipment. Depending on how the SC Hunley Commission and the Navy negotiate the programmatic agreement this may be provided from the federal government.

If the vessel can not be supplied from outside the state for whatever reason, then state resources will need to be used. SCIAA has approached the South Carolina Department of Natural Resources Division of Marine Resources to request their assistance in meeting these necessary requirements and to provide advice as to the procurement procedures to be followed.

Site Mapping

The *H. L. Hunley* and possible debris field associated with the site will need to be mapped using conventional underwater archaeology methods. This will entail establishing a baseline or baselines in practical locations in proximity to the debris field. The baselines will be permanently located using a Global Positioning System (GPS) unit and an as yet to be determined submerged datum. All horizontal measurements will be made relative to the baseline using triangulation or offset methods where appropriate. Temporary vertical datum points will also be established around the site and tied to the permanent points. These points will be used to plot and record the site. Assessments will be made regarding distribution patterns of the debris field, orientation

of the vessel and exposed stratigraphic layers and matrix to elucidate site transformation processes since the time of sinking.

If the structure of the *H. L. Hunley* is visible it will be recorded at two levels. First, a table of general scantlings, such as length and beam, and locations of construction features will be produced. Second, detailed measurements will be taken of important features such as plate, rivet and joinery patterns, the propeller blades, diving fins, conning towers, locations of seacocks, and areas of structural weakness or damage. The product of these tasks will be a preliminary site map and exterior plan of the submarine. This will yield information necessary for site assessment, answer specific management questions, and allow for a more accurate scope of work to be produced. This phase will be accompanied by preliminary sampling strategies to narrow the appropriate conservation and stabilization plans (refer to Conservation and Stabilization section, below).

Historical Research

Historical research and analysis of the vessel will be run concurrently with the underwater archaeology and conservation assessment and management phases of the project. The objectives of the historical phase are (1) to locate and research all relevant secondary and primary sources concerning the *Hunley* and the *Hunley* wreck site; (2) to assist in the identification of component parts of the vessel and artifacts associated with the site; (3) to prepare files on the individuals associated with the vessel, particularly the builders and members of the crew that were on board when it sank; (4) to assist in the analysis of certain significant historical questions concerning the vessel, such as what did it actually look like, technology of the submarine, and why the submarine sank. This will add a dimension not available through archaeological research and provide additional management data for the SCIAA and the SC Hunley Commission.

To carry out these responsibilities, historians involved with the project will need to create a working archive of all historical information obtained. The initial step will be the location of the relevant sources. No attempt will be made "to reinvent the wheel". The published works, particularly those by James Kloeppel (1987), Mark Ragan (1995), and Milton Perry (1965), contain in their bibliographies nearly all of the known published works as well as some of the unpublished documents and manu-scripts on the *H. L. Hunley*. Copies of the materials listed in these bibliographies will be obtained and placed in the archives. Nevertheless, these bibliogra-phies, like all bibliographies, are not complete. For example none of the above list Hannah M. Yates, *The Story of the Pioneer*; Richard K. Wills, "The Confederate Privateer Pioneer and the Development of American Submersible Watercraft" (1994); Mr. Wills' thesis at Texas A & M University on this sub-ject; and relevant articles in the *Encyclopedia of the Confederacy* (4 vols.). Finally, works published since the publication of the Kloeppel's, Perry's, and Ragan's books need to be examined. Robert Schneller, Jr's, *A Quest for Glory: A Bibliography of Rear Admiral John A. Dahlgren*, and Raimondo Luraghi's, *A History of the Confederate States Navy* are two examples.

Further work will be required to locate and identify other materials. This will involve an exami-nation of other published works (both secondary and primary) concerning the American Civil War, the history of technology, and other related histori-cal subjects found in libraries such as the Library of Congress, the Navy Department Library, and the Smithsonian. This will also involve a search through repositories for published materials. Some manu-scripts are included in Kloeppel's, Perry's, and Ragan's works, but others are known to exist. For example, there are unpublished materials concern-ing the *Hunley* in the Museum of the Confederacy, Richmond, Virginia; Emory University Library, Atlanta, Georgia; The City of Mobile Museum; and the University of North Carolina Library, Chapel Hill.

Other repositories need to be consulted for materials, particularly those that house collections of Confederate naval officers. The archives of the Confederate Navy Department were destroyed at the end of the war. This is why the *Official Records of the Union and Confederate Navies in the War of the Rebellion* include so few Confederate docu-ments. Nevertheless, there is a great deal of manu-script material available.

The practice of military and naval officers keep-ing possession of the records of their commands was fortunately followed in the Confederate service. The result is that even though most of the "official records" of the Navy Department were destroyed, copies of many of the records are available in vari-ous depositories. In addition, the Confederate naval

officers corps was small and most of them knew each other, especially those that were in the United States Navy before the war. They corresponded with each other, and it is conceivable that some of this correspondence contains information about the *H. L. Hunley*.

The same may well be true of army officers sta-tioned in Mobile and Charleston, but this number is much larger and therefore more difficult to research. The private papers of certain Union naval officers, particularly those of John Dahlgren should be examined. Dahlgren, in command of the South Atlantic Blockading Squadron when the *H. L. Hunley* was in Charleston has papers scattered in various repositories, particularly in the Library of Congress and Syracuse University, Syracuse, New York. The Portsmouth Shipyard Museum, Portsmouth, Virginia (which has in the journal of the William P. Williamson, Chief Engineer of the Confederate navy); the University of Virginia library (Matthew F. Maury papers); the Virginia Historical Society, Richmond; Duke University, Durham, North Carolina; Tulane University New Orleans; The University of Alabama Library, Tuscaloosa, Alabama, among others. One important collection is in private hands, that of John M. Brooke, Chief of the Confederate Bureau of Ordnance and Hydrography. The collection is in the hands of George M. Brooke, Jr., in Lexington, Virginia.

The most important single source for Confederate military and naval history is the National Archives, Washington, D. C. and the regional depositories. According to their bibliogra-phies, Kloeppel, Perry, and Ragan examined records in the National Archives, but not necessarily all doc-uments that might well have information on the *H. L. Hunley*. For example, none of these authors cite Record Group 365, which includes records of the Confederate Department of the Treasury. There is considerable naval material in these records, par-ticularly concerning shipbuilding.

Record Group 45 (Naval Records Collection of the Office of Naval Records and Library) is the most important single source for the Civil War. Many of these records were included in the published *Official Records*, but by no means all. Two large collections in this record group, not cited by the above authors, are the Confederate subject file and the area file. Fortunately most, but not all, of the National Archives material concerning the Civil War is avail-able on microfilm. Records of the Army Corps of

Engineers (RG77); records of amnesty and pardon (RG59), and records pertaining to Courts of Inquiry (RG125) are not microfilmed and need to be examined. Records of the US Army Corps of Engineers for Charleston can also be found in the regional depository at Eastpoint, Georgia. The Naval Historical Center, Washington Navy Yard, Washington, D. C. contains files on the *H. L. Hunley*, *USS Housatonic*, and officers associated with both the Confederate and Union navies.

Finally, genealogical research of the *H. L. Hunley*'s crew members, particularly those that were lost on her final voyage, will need to be done.

The Historical Importance of the *H. L. Hunley*

Technology is the application of engineering and science to practical purposes. The American Civil War, like all wars, clearly stimulated developments in technology. Bernard and Fawn Brodie (1962) wrote, "The American Civil War was a colossal proving ground for improving weapons of all kinds. For the first time, the achievements of the industrial and scientific revolution were used on a large scale in war." (pp. 133134). The submarine, particularly *H. L. Hunley*, was perhaps the most dramatic naval weapon introduced during the war.

The *H. L. Hunley* is recognized as the first successful submarine in history; the first submersible to actually sink a ship. As such, it represents a significant breakthrough in technology. It is also illustrative of Southern technological ingenuity, an ability to develop and produce weapons such as armored vessels, rifled guns, and of course, submersibles and semisubmersibles, a feat all the more remarkable considering the preeminent agrarian and agricultural nature of the South before the war. Admittedly, it was born out of necessity; the Confederacy had to industrialize in order to survive. It also had to be innovative if it was to successfully challenge the North, with its overwhelming superiority in economic and military might. The Confederacy was a small weak nation with no navy, and without the potential to keep pace with its opponent. Traditionally, the underdog or small power has resorted to new types of weapons and ships, and the Confederacy was no exception. Underseas weapons such as mines (torpedoes) and submersibles, including the *H. L. Hunley*, were a product of this concept.

Data on Confederate naval technology, such as builder's plans, accurate drawings, photographs, detailed specifications, shipbuilding methodologies and materials, are extremely scarce. For that reason, the examination and recovery of the underwater remains of Confederate naval weapons such as the *H. L. Hunley* is extremely important. Through underwater archaeology, scholars will be able to obtain the necessary research information to understand Confederate naval technology.

Conservation and Stabilization

The conservation of the *H. L. Hunley* will be a complex, expensive, and time consuming task. This requires that careful attention be paid to the published standards of practice and ethics, and the present realities of conservation science. There will be only one opportunity to do the conservation of the *H. L. Hunley* correctly. Several of these points are developed further and addressed briefly below. In addition, five possible conservation management plans are presented as requested by the SC Hunley Commission. The final determination as to which management plan can be implemented rests on the base data discussed in previous sections, the financial solvency of the groups involved, and the consensus of the public and agencies who are mandated with the vessel's stewardship.

Discussion

NUMA recently provided the Navy with the vessel's coordinates, and they have in turn passed them on to the SC Hunley Commission. Once the Commission makes this location available to the SCIAA–HPWG, it will be necessary to carefully coordinate the project's specific support logistics to that point. It is possible that the unique characteristics of that location may modify the management plan in presently unforeseen ways.

Regardless of its specific location, the *H. L. Hunley* is in a precarious balance with its surroundings. Iron is acutely sensitive to wet environments. The speed and depth of iron corrosion in sea water is dependent on several factors. These factors include the available oxygen at the ironmoisture film interface, the presence and availability of chloride ions to the metal, electrical conductivity, water velocity, temperature, biological fouling of the surfaces and the presence of sulfate reducing bacteria, mechanical stress, pollution, silt and suspended sediments, and the formation of differential chemical films.

The *H. L. Hunley* has been on the bottom of the ocean for 131 years. Charleston Harbor's shifting sands and silts, resulting from wave and storm action, are well known and documented. This situation coupled with the shallow depths of the targeted areas, and the first hand experience of SCIAA research divers, clearly identifies a dynamic environment. There can be no doubt that these factors have contributed to the vessel's current condition.

The probable effects of periods of high and low oxygen, temperature fluctuations, abrasion and biological fouling of the intermittently and incompletely exposed vessel's surfaces, scouring of derived stable or at least less active chemical films by suspended silt and sediments, and the concomitant shifts in electrical conductivity and galvanic damage throughout the length of the vessel should give everyone involved with this project reason to pause and reflect. In addition, the dissolved chemical pollutants from upstream farm, residential, and industrial users coupled with the usual outflows of a commercial and military port must be taken into account.

During the Congressional Hearings for Representative Mark Sanford's bill it was suggested by several speakers that marine artifacts may be removed from their locations and indefinitely stored in identical or at least similar environments without incurring damage. Unfortunately, this is not really the case. It is not possible to produce identical or even similar environments for complex artifacts. Any change in the environment will cause changes in the vessel itself. These changes are cumulative and must be monitored with care as part of an overall conservation plan. Once an artifact has been disturbed it will seek a new equilibrium. The extent that the artifact must change to reach the new balance determines the depth and extent of what may be new damage. The greater the disturbance, the greater the change, with the end result a greater risk of damage; unless carefully managed. This reality must be kept in mind at all times.

No accurate plans exist for the *H. L. Hunley*. Nonetheless, a careful reading of the historic record provides valuable details, subject to verification (refer to Historical Research; and, Archaeology and Survey), that are essential to the successful production and implementation of conservation plans.

Present research suggests several important points. First, the vessel is a complex composite artifact composed of wrought iron, cast iron, brass, glass, rubber, and textiles. Second, the thinness of the vessel's skin, and the insetting of the attaching rivets, is cause for grave concern about the structural integrity of the vessel. Third, the cramped interior space of the submarine will make conservation and stabilization of interior corrosion difficult. Fourth, the disparate metals used to make the vessel are subject to galvanic deterioration and require careful attention to their individual properties. Fifth, archaeological excavations conducted by SCIAA in areas bordering Charleston Harbor resulted in the recovery of textiles and rubber from the same time period. These materials may have survived aboard this vessel as well. Finally, pseudomorphs, fragile fossilized castings of organic materials, may exist in the corrosion of the stuffing boxes and in other areas. These will need to be identified, recorded, and preserved.

Wrought iron is one of the worst metals to conserve from an ocean environment. It is readily attacked by sea water and looses surface details quickly and irrevocably. Cast iron is only a little better and forms graphite rich corrosion layers around the remaining metal core in sea water. This graphite layer often preserves surface details, but has only an illusory strength and is easily lost. Great care must be used to make sure that the transfer of the artifact from the sea to its storage/treatment tank is seamless in execution. If this is not done then the risk of damage is great. In the case of cast iron, the strong heat produced by renewed corrosion between the iron and graphite layers can result in spalling and disintegration.

There are no treatments for iron artifacts recovered from the sea that are 100% effective or safe. The efficacy of a treatment is a complex interaction of the artifact, its unique history and needs, and the chosen regimen with its areas of success and shortcomings. All the methods discussed can be used effectively, but will result in differing levels of physical damage and loss of data. In each case, benefits must be weighed against problems that are, in some cases, a result of the treatments themselves.

Present techniques include washings, desiccation, alkaline sulfite reduction, hydrogen reduction, and electrolysis. Under certain optimum conditions each of these techniques has provided at least satisfactory results. Unfortunately, artifacts from the sea floor rarely exhibit uniform or optimum conditions, and in the specific case of the *H. L. Hunley* this is extremely unlikely.

Washing iron artifacts in chemical solutions or freshwater is very common. The primary intent is to remove highly reactive chloride ions (Cl–) deposited in the metal from the sea water. Minimally intrusive depending on the chemical used, this technique is reasonably effective in removing chloride from exterior layers of cast iron. Unfortunately, it is less effective at depth and limited to chloride products soluble in the solvent being used. The result is an artifact that, more often than not, harbors considerable chloride compounds and traces of the washing solution. These compounds and imported chemicals continue to deteriorate the metal, although at a slower pace then before. Washing is rarely done by itself. Instead, it is usually combined with one of several reduction techniques.

Desiccation, as its name suggests, focuses on the removal of moisture from the iron to halt corrosion. Dewatering using solvents, such as acetone, or through packing with silica gel, is a cost effective method for slowing destructive interactions. When the relative humidity falls below 20%, further corrosion of iron is unlikely. Unfortunately, it does not remove chlorides or other harmful chemicals that may be present, nor does it provide long term protection. When the available humidity approaches 40–60%, corrosion reoccurs. In addition, the shrinking of corrosion layers by the removal of mechanical and chemical water vapor, and the formation of salt crystals from residual trapped chloride, may damage their coherence and results in friable surfaces and a loss of information. Nonetheless, desiccation is used as an important step in more comprehensive processes that address the areas of concern.

Alkaline sulfite reduction is a technique that was designed to aid iron artifacts in shedding accumulated chlorides. The treatment requires the full immersion of the iron in an atmospherically sealed, heated, tank for several months. After which time, the object is washed and the chlorides found in the spent washing solution are measured. The washings continue until an appropriate chloride level is reached. After which, the cleaned artifact is preserved and protected using several possible techniques.

Alkaline sulfite reduction is thought to increase the pores in the corrosion layers. This in turn increases the surface area reached by the chemical wash and a greater quantity of chloride ions are removed from the artifact. This assumption has been challenged and the suitability of the treatment questioned fairly recently. In addition, the chemicals

used for the treatment are toxic, require careful detoxification before they can be disposed, are moderately expensive, and can produce poison gas under certain circumstances. Traditionally, this treatment has been used only on small artifacts.

There are two hydrogen reduction processes. The first is the Swedish process which results in the burning off of chlorides and the reduction of iron oxides (rust) to metallic iron. To do this, the artifact is heated within an electrical furnace through which a nitrogen/hydrogen mixture is pumped. This gas stream, at a temperature of 840°C, held for 24 hours, followed by a short period at 1060°C, produces a reduced metal surface with little remaining chlorides. The finished artifact can be quite remarkable for its detail.

Unfortunately, there are several problems with this process. First, it is really only effective on small artifacts. Second, it wipes out practically all information on the metallurgical processes that were used. Third, it works best with artifacts that contain less than 3% chloride (previous artifacts recovered from Charleston Harbor tested much higher). Fourth, spontaneous oxidation has occurred on artifacts that contained more than 3% chloride after they were removed from the furnace. And finally, low temperature melting of iron artifacts has been reported with this process, resulting in a total loss.

The Australian hydrogen reduction technique is an advance over the Swedish as it rectifies the problems of higher chlorides, spontaneous oxidation, and the loss of metallurgical data. In this treatment, several phases are introduced. First, the object is heated to drive off water vapor, then it is heated in pure hydrogen for 48 hours at 400°C, followed by slow cooling with a switch to nitrogen gas at 100°C until room temperature is reached. The cooled artifact is immediately placed in a sodium hydroxide solution and goes through several wash cycles until the residual chlorides are reduced to an appropriate level.

While clearly an advance over the first technique, there are still some problems attached to this treatment. As before, it is only effective on relatively small artifacts. Second, it is very slow. Third, several of the chemicals used are dangerous. And fourth, the use of hydrogen gas is dangerous in and of itself and can result in catastrophic explosions. Finally, hydrogen furnaces have been proven to be significantly expensive to maintain and operate.

Electrolysis is the most commonly used technique for treating marine iron. As its name implies, this treatment uses a mild current running through the artifact as it rests in an electrolyte bath between two anodes. The process reduces corrosion, aids in the removal of chlorides, and makes it much easier to remove stubborn concretions and scale. The electrolyte usually consists of sodium carbonate or sodium hydroxide dissolved in water. Sodium hydroxide is the preferred technical solution.

While considerably safer and cheaper than alkaline sulfite reduction or hydrogen furnaces, and comparatively successful in the removal of chlorides, this technique has several drawbacks. First, sodium hydroxide, lye, while safer than the other techniques still poses health and environmental risks. Second, the alternative solution, sodium carbonate, can result in the precipitation of insoluble carbonates on the metal at higher concentrations, which the requires extensive hand cleaning. Third, the pioneering work from Western Australia strongly suggests that wrought iron and cast iron should never be electrolyzed in the same tank. This is a serious problem for the treatment of the combined cast and wrought elements of the *H. L. Hunley* by this method. It should be noted, however, that many American conservators have ignored this internationally recognized tenet with mixed results. Fourth, cast iron artifacts must be electrolyzed separately to control selective treatment induced destruction of the artifact surfaces (exfoliation). And finally, in many instances significant loss of surface detail occurs with this technique. This results in the production of a significantly damaged, "false face" that has little connection to the original surface.

Regardless of which technique or techniques are chosen for this project, conservation is a complex process that requires a commitment to the highest standards of the profession. The chemical, physical, historic, and aesthetic properties of the artifact must be fully considered prior to any intrusive actions. This is given a greater urgency as numerous well meaning individuals and groups have stepped forward and volunteered to do the vessel's conservation. In several instances, they have come armed with outdated "how to manuals" that were produced in the 1960s and 70s. Mainstream conservation is a scientific discipline that is not related to Betty Crocker®. There is no standard recipe and each artifact must be dealt with on its own peculiar terms by qualified, vetted professionals.

Conservation Management Plans

None of the following management plans should be implemented prior to an indepth analyses of the vessel while it is on the ocean floor. It is strongly suggested that adequate analyses should include, but are not be limited to, the following activities.

1.) A legal verification that the NUMA find is the *H. L. Hunley*.
2.) Mapping of the site and possible debris field.
3.) Sampling the sediments overlying and near the vessel for chemical composition.
4.) Nonintrusive mapping of the vessel by remote sensing equipment, such as a high resolution bottom profiler.
5.) Determination of the structural integrity of the vessel.
6.) Identification of decomposition materials adhering to the outer hull of the vessel.

In addition to the above, the following personnel and support must be identified:

7.) Designation of the conservation treatment facility and trained staff.
8.) Designation of trained marine transports.
9.) Designation of certified/licensed Ocean Engineer.
10.) Designation of exhibiting agency.
11.) Identification of funds for:
    a) archaeology
    b) conservation
    c) salvage
    d) transport
    e) exhibition
    f) maintenance.

The information gathered by these analyses and activities are essential, cannot be deferred, and must be accomplished prior to other work. Once this information is obtained it should be used to modify and identify the most appropriate conservation management plan. Some of the items on this list fall within the management scope of the SCIAA and have been addressed earlier. Several others will fall to the successful contractor to perform under SCIAA and federal technical oversight. In addition, two national advisory groups have been approached by SCIAA to assist the agency in this process through consultation, and recommendations.

The American Institute for Conservation of Historic and Artistic Works (AIC) has convened an Advisory Panel to the Hunley Project at the request of the SCIAA Hunley Project Working Group

(HPWG). The panel's role is to act as an advisor to the HPWG, critique conservation and analysis plans, provide additional professional perspectives, and to act as a sounding board. Its responsibilities are strictly advisory. The membership of the panel has been left to the discretion of the AIC, with the understanding that individuals named to the panel will meet the highest levels of academic and professional experience in archaeological conservation.

The Advisory Council for Underwater Archaeology (ACUA), which operates under the aegis of the Society for Historical Archaeology has also been approached to assist in the process by SCIAA. While expressing interest, no formal advisory board has yet to be impaneled.

There are five possible paths that the conservation or stabilization process may follow. These plans are presented here in order of least intrusive and expensive to most intrusive and expensive as requested by the SC Hunley Commission. In that order they are: 1) the vessel is left in place with minimal conservation or stabilization; 2) the vessel is left in place with conservation or stabilization; 3) if in pieces, portions of the vessel are removed and conserved with minimal preservation of the remains in place; 4) if in pieces, portions of the vessel are removed and conserved with preservation of the remains in place; and, 5) the vessel is recovered and conserved. Each of these plans will be discussed briefly below with attention to their positive and negative points. In the interest of clarity a summary statement concerning time, monitoring, and personnel follows each scenario. In several, but not all, instances the activities are concurrent.

1. Vessel in Place, Minimal Conservation or Stabilization: This plan assumes that the *H. L. Hunley* will be found to be not only too fragile to salvage, but so deteriorated that only a minimal expenditure of funds are warranted. Minimal expenditures might entail additional protective covering of the wreck to attempt to preserve the remains for future, and hopefully more advanced, recovery and conservation techniques.

No specific conservation facility or additional conservation personnel will be necessary for the implementation of this plan. Consultation with an ocean engineer is suggested for identification of protective coverings, if warranted.

Time:

Archaeology and Conservation Assessment, 18 months.

2. Vessel in Place, Conservation and Stabilization: This plan assumes that the *H. L. Hunley* will be found to be too fragile to remove, but preserveable in place on the ocean floor. This may be accomplished several different ways. First, sacrificial anodes may be produced and attached to the vessel to halt further corrosion. Second, ocean engineered buffering systems may be erected to better protect the vessel from harmful conditions, as identified through the assessment phase. Finally, close monitoring of the above will produce additional data that may suggest other creative solutions. As before, the intent is to preserve the remains for the future when more advanced, recovery and conservation techniques may be available.

This plan requires the designation of diving personnel for placement/replacement of the possible anode protection and to assess the continuing state of the *H. L. Hunley*; a dive tender to ferry the monitoring personnel to the site; and an archaeological objects conservator to supervise, assess and implement conservation activities. Standard dive safety procedures require two certified divers down, one on deck as standby, and a captain/pilot for the dive tender. At least one of the divers should be trained as a conservation technician or as a full conservator. No specific conservation facility is necessary for this plan, although at least the contractual services of an archaeological objects conservator must be secured. The dive tender may be rented, contracted with the divers, or bought outright.

Time:

Archaeology and Initial Conservation Assessment, 18 months.

Monitoring:

On site: quarterly, in perpetuity.

Personnel:

Four divers (at least one trained in conservation).

3. Portions Recovered and Conserved, Minimal Intervention of In Situ Remains: This plan assumes that the *H. L. Hunley* will be found in several pieces with significant sections of the vessel available for safe recovery, and other pieces too deteriorated and fragile to be disturbed. The portion remaining on the ocean floor will be dealt with as stated in plan 1. The recovered portions will need to be handled in an extremely careful and coordinated fashion as set out below.

First, depending on size and shape, specially constructed lifting slings and supports will need to be fashioned to buffer the recoverable sections from as much stress as possible during the lift. Second, the lifting cradles should be constructed from materials that allow for artifact support throughout the conservation process. Third, if the recovered sections are small, then they can be treated in the existing conservation area at the Charleston Museum or, if several in number and of sufficient strength and integrity, at the SCIAA Facility located in Columbia. Nonetheless, all efforts should be made to handle the conservation at the Charleston Museum, if possible. Fourth, if the sections are large, or the process determined to be the most beneficial requires special equipment, then a separate treatment area close to the final exhibit area will need to be built and furnished. Fifth, the storage or exhibition of the recovered sections will require specially designed cases or rooms with inert atmospheres, humidity control, monitoring equipment, environmental backup, emergency power, and safe emergency access. Sixth, three additional trained staff will need to be hired either prior to conservation, or at the very least, prior to exhibit construction. Seventh, specially trained staff will need to oversee the monitoring of the vessel sections once they are on display in perpetuity. Finally, a disaster preparedness plan that specifically addresses the vessel will need to be produced by the exhibiting institution.

Time:

Archaeology and Initial Conservation Assessment, 18 months.

Laboratory Conservation, 8 months to 36 months.

Design and Testing of Environmental exhibit cases, 6 months.

Environmental exhibit hall, 3 to 5 years.

Conservation Facility, 6 months to 1 year.

Monitoring:

Exhibit case(s) or hall: twice daily, in perpetuity.

Personnel:

Four to six divers plus two conservators and two technicians (dependent on quantity of materials recovered).

4. Portions Recovered and Conserved, In Situ Remains Stabilized: This plan assumes that the *H. L. Hunley* will have significant sections of the vessel available for safe recovery with a fragile, preservable section in place on the ocean floor. The materials left in place will be handled as stated in Plan 2. The materials removed for conservation will be handled as stated in Plan 3. This significantly

increases perpetual expenses due to the need to monitor difficult materials in two locations under specialized circumstances.

Time:

Archaeology and Initial Conservation Assessment, 18 months.

Laboratory Conservation, 8 months to 36 months.

Environmental exhibit cases, 6 months.

Environmental exhibit hall, 3 to 5 years.

Conservation Facility, 6 months to 1 year.

Monitoring:

Ocean: quarterly, in perpetuity.

Exhibit case(s) or hall: twice daily, in perpetuity.

Personnel:

Four to six divers plus two conservators and two technicians (dependent on quantity of materials recovered).

5. Vessel Recovered and Conserved: This plan assumes that the *H. L. Hunley* will be determined to be in a remarkable state of preservation that will allow it to be safely raised from the ocean floor. The recovered vessel will need to be handled in an extremely careful and coordinated fashion as set out below.

First, an ocean engineering firm with appropriate specialized equipment, and documented experience in difficult, technical recoveries will need to be identified and hired. Second, specially constructed lifting slings and supports must be fashioned to buffer the recoverable vessel from as much stress as possible during the lift. Third, the lifting cradles must be constructed from materials that allow for artifact support throughout the conservation process. Fourth, the support cradles must be engineered to not impede the chosen conservation process. Fifth, the vessel must be treated in either a separate treatment area close to the final exhibit area, or within the final exhibit area. In either case this treatment center/exhibit area must be carefully designed, built, and furnished. Sixth, the possibility that the untreated vessel will be able to travel anywhere outside the Charleston area is slim to none. Seventh, the final storage or exhibition of the treated vessel will require specially designed cases or rooms with inert atmospheres, humidity control, monitoring equipment, environmental backup, emergency power, and safe emergency access. Eighth, additional trained staff will need to be hired by the facility prior to conservation. Ninth, specially trained staff will need to oversee the monitoring of the vessel once it is on display in perpetuity. Finally, a disaster preparedness plan that specifically addresses the vessel will need to be produced by the exhibiting institution.

Time:

Archaeology and Initial Conservation Assessment, 18 months.

Laboratory Conservation, 3 to 10 years.

Environmental exhibit hall, 3 to 5 years.

Conservation Facility, 6 months to 1 year.

Monitoring:

Exhibit case(s) or hall: twice daily, in perpetuity.

Personnel:

Four to six divers plus two conservators and two technicians. At least one conservator and one technician will need to oversee the exhibit in perpetuity.

Conservation Summary

Wise use and proactive stewardship require a very careful weighing of the benefits and detriments of the available conservation techniques. Promises should not be made that present science can not keep; nor should undue haste take the place of considered actions. Under most circumstances, the first conservation attempt is the only attempt.

Identification and Preservation of Human Remains

The *H. L. Hunley* is not only a vessel of historical significance, it is also a war grave. On 17 February, 1864, nine volunteers lost their lives in the pursuit of their beliefs while engaged in a new form of warfare. Public sensitivity to the historic and political realities that still surround these events must be taken into account, as well as the direct wishes of any surviving descendants yet to be identified. Balancing the needs and expectations of the public, descendants, and the scientific community could become a complex undertaking. This can be avoided by the adoption of a unified action plan that balances the needs and sensibilities of the groups involved. The Hunley Project Working Group, in keeping with the published burial policy of the South Carolina Institute of Archaeology and Anthropology as the state's steward for archaeological burials, presents the following methodology and management plan.

Methodology

The methodology for the identification and

preservation of the human remains encompasses four distinct disciplines within the scientific community. They are archaeology, forensic anthropology, conservation, and history. In addition, political and personal issues must be incorporated and will mitigate the level of interaction by the management agency with the human remains and the ultimate direction of any scientific analyses. This latter point is the provenience of the SC Hunley Commission, and other interested parties, and is left to them to decide. The scientific areas are outlined below.

Archaeology: The management, recovery, identification, and preservation of human remains from underwater sites has been a common undertaking of the South Carolina Institute of Archaeology and Anthropology and its Underwater Archaeology Division for the last twenty years, as legally mandated by the South Carolina Underwater Antiquities Act (revised 1991). The Underwater Archaeology Division research dive team uses standard archaeological techniques. These include gridding and mapping of the debris field and vessel interior, hand excavation of features, judicious and careful use of assisted excavation techniques when warranted (e.g., air lift), in place recording, photographic recording techniques (e.g., montage, still, and video), computer assisted drafting, and three dimensional computer modeling. In addition, the dive team is experienced in the recovery of very small items, such as seed beads, through the use of secondary sifting techniques and flotation. Given the expected nature of the wreck, the personal items believed to have been carried by the crew, and the uniqueness of the vessel, all of these techniques will be used. Careful integration of this mandated area by the managing agency with the successful contractor is a must.

Forensics: Dr. Ted Rathbun, Deputy State Archaeologist for Forensics, conducts and oversees all analyses of archaeological human remains for the South Carolina Institute of Archaeology and Anthropology, Office of the State Archaeologist. He has thirty one years of experience in the field, is board certified by the American Board of Forensic Anthropology, and a Fellow of the American Academy of Forensic Science. He is internationally acclaimed for his work and is a civilian consultant to the Joint Chiefs of Staff. On this project he will personally conduct the analysis and identification of any and all human remains recovered.

The suggested identification and analysis of the

human remains encompasses several activities. These are outlined below.

1. After desalination, stabilization, and reconstruction of the skeletal materials and fragments (see Conservation below), the standard scientific determination of sex, age, ancestry, and stature will be determined following forensic protocol. Although all the crew members were recorded as male, for the study to be scientifically valid this determination may not be skipped.

2. Specific identities for the crew's remains will be made if possible. This aspect of the forensic research is heavily dependent on supplementary documentation (see History sections). It entails finding and acquiring military, medical, family, and contemporary antemortem records that identify physical characteristics that survive in the skeleton. Photographs, and even paintings, have their use, as the application of electronic videosuperimposition allows the placement of the individuals face and head over a surviving skull. This in turn assists in the inclusion or exclusion of the skeletal remains as being likely to have come from the person depicted in the photograph or painting.

3. If sufficient facial and cranial bones survive and are stable, then forensic facial reproductions can be produced. These can be made even if the documentary evidence for the crews features are lacking. Forensic facial reproductions allow for the possible identification of crew members in records not directly tied to the *Hunley*, and provide a record of the probable facial features of the crew for educational and exhibit purposes. A high quality specialized cast of the reconstructed cranial and facial bones will be made, which in turn produces the base for the reproduction. The skeletal materials themselves are unharmed and freed for reinterment or additional study.

4. Biohistorical and scientific questions for this time period are receiving increased attention from the scientific community. Even if specific identification can not be accomplished, the crew's remains provide an important "window to the past." Data concerning health, disease, activity patterns, and pathology will be acquired from the basic analysis and will be compared with previous work by the South Carolina Institute of Archaeology and Anthropology, and others, at Folly Island, S. C.; Charleston Confederate Naval Cemetery at the Citadel, S. C.; Remley Plantation near Charleston, S. C.; and, Confederate troops at Gioretta Pass,

New Mexico. Other collections will be included as they are identified.

Conservation: The South Carolina Institute of Archaeology and Anthropology routinely recovers and conserves skeletal materials. At the present time, the bones recovered from the *H. L. Hunley* are expected to be conserved by the SCIAA, not the successful contractor, and only at a level that ensures stability during study. The extent to which these remains will be conserved beyond basic stability is dependent upon the wishes and plans of the SC Hunley Commission in consultation with other appropriate parties.

Vertebrate skeletal materials are composed of a protein, ossein, a collagen fiber, and hydroxyapatite, a crystalline inorganic composed of calcium phosphate, carbonate, and fluoride. Collagen fibrils form the connective structure of the bone and are surrounded by the hydroxyapatite, which provides rigidity and strength. The ratio for these materials in adult bone is 1:2, collagen to hydroxyapatite. Preservation of collagen and hydroxyapatite is complicated by the fact that they survive best at polar opposites of pH. Acidic conditions or deposits attack the hydroxyapatite, and alkaline ones attack the collagen. In addition, bacteria selectively attack the collagen structurally weakening the bone. The ocean environment can be, generally speaking, an excellent preserver of skeletal materials. There is every reason to expect skeletal material either in the vessel or in the surrounding debris field.

The conservation and treatment of skeletal materials is well established and successful. Desalination of the bone is essential for removal of soluble salt deposited from the sea water. Salt is hygroscopic, aids in the production of acids that attack the hydroxyapatite component, and can cause severe damage to delicate remains if allowed to crystallize during drying. Desalination is done through a series of distilled water baths that are checked for leached salt content. The baths are stopped when the appropriate dissolved salt level is reached.

Once the bone is desalinated, and if it is the wish of the SC Hunley Commission, then it may be stabilized in preparation for reconstruction and analysis. Public documentation and scientific publication of all decisions and results from the conservation process in the appropriate refereed conservation journals is essential.

History: Placing human remains within their

full context relies heavily on documentary materials. Military records of enlistment, requests by widows and surviving dependents for assistance, medical and dental records, photographs, paintings, and family and contemporary descriptions, and other historical accounts provide invaluable clues and data. All extant records of these types for the nine crew members known to have been on the *H. L. Hunley*'s last voyage will be sought, identified, and analyzed. This undertaking, as with all historic research, falls under the provenience of the CoPrincipal Investigator for History, Dr. William Still. The derived data will be useful for all phases of the project, from field work and assessment through exhibit and public education. In addition, several members of the Commission and general public have come forward with valuable information concerning the crew from their private research. These materials will be evaluated and incorporated as well.

Management Plan and Discussion

The SC Hunley Commission, in consultation with other appropriate groups, must make the determination as to what level it wishes the scientific analyses of the human remains to proceed. The previous section outlines several activities and tasks available to the Commission that they may decide not to do. The disciplines of archaeology, forensic anthropology, and conservation are acutely aware that the violation of sepulcher requires no less than the highest reasons for that action. All Institute activities necessary to fulfill the Commission's mandate concerning the grave site will go before the Institute's internal Burial Policy Committee for additional comment and advice. The findings of that committee will be presented to the Chair of the Commission for his final review.

There are four possible paths that the recovery and identification process may follow. These plans are presented here in order of least intrusive and expensive to most intrusive and expensive. In that order they are: 1) the human remains are left on the vessel or within the debris field, as a protected grave site; 2) the human remains are recovered from the vessel or debris field and reinterred without additional study or intervention; 3) the human remains are recovered from the vessel or debris field, stabi-lized, analyzed, and reinterred 4) the human remains are recovered from the vessel or debris field, stabilized, analyzed, and become an honored part of the state's collections.

The least viable or likely of these options is number four. The inclusion of the crew's remains as a part of a state or federal skeletal research collection could only be accomplished through broad public support and the specific approval of any descendants, which seems very unlikely.

Forensics Summary

Prudent planning calls for the expectation of the recovery of human remains from the *H. L. Hunley*. Conversations with members of the press and public suggest that there may be a general expectation that the crew members bodies are fully intact and recoverable. This is unfortunately not the case as the softtissues have melted away long ago. Nonetheless, the fanciful belief has benefited the project through the generation of public excitement and enthusiasm.

The determination of the depth and nature of the scientific analyses that will be done on the crew members' remains is the provenience of the SC Hunley Commission in consultation with other appropriate parties. A great deal of information may be acquired through these studies that is unobtainable by any other means. Undoubtedly, the Commission will hold public hearings on the matter, and the SCIAA Hunley Project Working Group looks forward to explaining to the interested public the benefits of collaborative forensic research.

Prepared February 5, 1996 by the SCIAA Hunley Project Working Group:

Mr. Christopher F. Amer, Archaeology
Dr. Jonathan M. Leader, Conservation
Dr. William N. Still, History
Ms. B. Lynn Harris, Archaeology
Dr. Ted Rathbun, Forensic Anthropology

CHRONOLOGY

1823

December 29: Horace Lawson Hunley is born in Sumner County, Tennessee. At the outbreak of the war he is a successful sugar broker and the deputy collector of customs in New Orleans.

1861

April 12: Confederate batteries bombard Fort Sumter in Charleston Harbor, signaling the start of the Civil War.

Summer: New Orleans machine shop owners James McClintock and Baxter Watson begin work in earnest on a three-man submarine, the *Pioneer*. Horace Hunley is a principal financial backer.

1862

February: The *Pioneer* is successfully tested in the New Basin Canal and Lake Pontchartrain.

March 31: Owners of the *Pioneer* are granted a letter of marque from the Confederate government, allowing them to operate the vessel as a privateer.

April: The fall of New Orleans to the Union army forces Hunley, McClintock and Watson to scuttle the *Pioneer* in the New Basin Canal and to relocate to Mobile, Alabama.

Summer-Fall: A second experimental submarine, wholly funded by Hunley and alternately called the *Pioneer II* and the *American Diver*, is built at the Park and Lyons machine shop in Mobile.

1863

February: The *Pioneer II* has several trial runs in Mobile Bay. One day it sinks in heavy seas while being towed to Fort Morgan. The crew escapes but the vessel is irretrievably lost.

Spring-Summer: Hunley becomes a one-third shareholder in the Singer Submarine Corps, an organization started by mechanical engineer E. C. Singer to underwrite the cost of a third experimental submarine. Under the direction of McClintock and Lieutenant William A. Alexander the *H. L. Hunley* is built.

July 31: The *Hunley* successfully sinks a flat boat in a demonstration on the Mobile River.

August 7: The *Hunley* is ordered to be moved by train to Charleston, South Carolina, where it is intended to be used against the blockading U. S. fleet. It arrives a week later.

August 23: Upset by the seeming timidity of the *Hunley*'s civilian owners, military authorities in Charleston seize the vessel and replace its crew with volunteers from the Confederate navy. The sub, now officially known as the *CSS H. L. Hunley*, is commanded by Lieutenant John A. Payne.

August 29: An inexperienced crew causes the *Hunley* to accidentally submerge during a training mission near Fort Johnson in Charleston Harbor. Five of the nine crew members drown. Two weeks later the *Hunley* is salvaged.

September 19: Hunley successfully requests that the submarine be placed under his control and that he be allowed to furnish it with an experienced crew from Mobile.

October 15: The *Hunley*, piloted by Captain Hunley, goes into an inadvertent dive during a training mission and plows bow-first to the bottom of Charleston harbor. All eight hands, including the *Hunley*'s namesake, die.

November 7: The *Hunley* is brought back to the surface. The bodies of Hunley and his crew are buried at Charleston's Magnolia Cemetery.

November 12: Lieutenant George A. Dixon requests to be put in command of the *Hunley*. The submarine is outfitted with a fresh crew of volunteers, including five men from the *CSS Indian Chief*.

1864

February 17: After several weeks of training and tests, the *Hunley* is ordered to attack the *USS Housatonic*. At about 8:45 P.M. on a clear, moonlit night, the *Hunley* detonates a torpedo against the blockader's hull, sinking the ship and causing five deaths. In the process of completing the first successful submarine attack in the history of warfare, the *Hunley* and its entire crew are lost.

February 26: The U. S. Navy convenes a board of inquiry into the *Housatonic*'s sinking. The court's conclusion is that it was "blown up and sunk by a rebel torpedo craft."

February 29: The sinking of the *Housatonic* is reported for the first time in Charleston newspapers.

1865

February 17: Exactly one year after the *Hunley*'s sinking of the *Housatonic*, Charleston falls.

1870

October 8: A Charleston newspaper erroneously reports that divers have found the wreck of the *Hunley* lying next to the sunken hull of the *Housatonic*. Speculation over the submarine's exact fate and the location of its wreck will continue for well over a century.

1873

Summer: The rotting superstructure of the *Housatonic*, a nuisance to navigation since its sinking, is demolished and the vessel moved to a new position in deeper water off Sullivan's Island.

1909

February-March: The remaining wreckage of the *Housatonic* is surveyed and then dynamited to a more acceptable level, allowing navigation over its hull. Over the next several decades its final resting place is covered by sand and forgotten.

1980

Summer: Noted underwater explorer Clive Cussler launches his first of several attempts to find the *Hunley*. In conjunction with the National Underwater & Marine Agency, a nonprofit organization, the expedition locates the wreck site of the *Housatonic*. Concurrently, underwater archeologist Edward Lee Spence files papers in Federal District Court to secure ownership and salvage rights to the *Hunley* and *Housatonic*, which he claims to have discovered ten years earlier.

1991

March 25: The Sons of Confederate Veterans posthumously awards each member of the final crew of the *Hunley* the Medal of Honor of the Confederate States of America. Caldwell Delaney, director of the Museum of the City of Mobile, accepts the award on their behalf.

1995

May 11: Cussler announces the May 3, 1995 discovery of the *Hunley* several miles outside Charleston Harbor, lying in thirty feet of water at the approach to Moffitt's Channel.
September 14. Edward Lee Spence donates ownership rights to the *Hunley* to the State of South Carolina.

2000

August 8: After spending the last 136 years submerged in sand and water, the *Hunley* is raised to the surface.

BIBLIOGRAPHY

William A. Alexander. "The Confederate Submarine Torpedo Boat *Hunley*." *Gulf States Historical Magazine* (September 1902).

———. "Thrilling Chapter in the History of the Confederate States Navy." *Southern Historical Society Papers*. Vol. XXX (Jan.-Dec. 1902).

———. "The Heroes of the *Hunley*." *Munsey Magazine* (August 1903).

Bern Anderson. *By Sea and by River: The Naval History of the Civil War*. New York: Knopf, 1962.

Ben L. Bassham. *Conrad Wise Chapman: Artist and Soldier of the Civil War*. Kent, Ohio: Kent State University Press, 1998.

P. G. T. Beauregard. "Torpedo Service in the Harbor and Water Defense of Charleston." *Southern Historical Society Papers*. Vol. V (April 1878).

Arthur W. Bergeron. *Confederate Mobile*. Jackson: University Press of Mississippi, 1991.

C. H. Blair. "Submarines of the Confederate Navy." *U. S. Naval Institute Proceedings* (October 1952).

Louis H. Bolander. "The *Alligator*, First Federal Submarine of the Civil War." *U. S. Naval Institute Proceedings* (June 1938).

B. Bowman. "The *Hunley*: Ill-fated Confederate Submarine." *Civil War History* (September 1959).

"Builder of First Submarine Dead." *Mobile Register* (May 14, 1914).

E. Milby Burton. *The Siege of Charleston, 1861-1865*. Columbia: University of South Carolina Press, 1970.

R. Thomas Campbell. *Southern Fire: Naval Exploits of the Confederacy*. Shippensburg, Pa.: White Mane, 1997.

———. *Fire and Thunder: Exploits of the Confederate States Navy*. Shippensburg, Pa.: White Mane, 1998.

The Civil War at Charleston. Charleston, S.C.: Evening Post Publishing, 1973.

P. C. Coker III. *Charleston's Maritime Heritage, 1670–1865*. Charleston, S.C.: CokerCraft Press, 1987.

Wilbur Cross. "The Last Chance." *Civil War* (December 1998).

Clive Cussler. *The Sea Hunters: True Adventures with Famous Shipwrecks*. New York: Simon & Schuster, 1996.

Burke Davis. *Our Incredible Civil War*. New York: Ballantine, 1974.

William C. Davis. *The Cause Lost: Myths and Realities of the Confederacy*. Lawrence: University Press of Kansas, 1996.

———. *Duel Between the First Ironclads*. New York: Doubleday, 1975.

James Tertius deKay. *Monitor: The Story of the Legendary Civil War Ironclad and the Man Whose Invention Changed the Course of History*. New York: Walker & Co., 1997.

"Dixon, Builder of the Submarine *Hunley*, Went to Death in the Deep." *Mobile Daily Herald* (November 15, 1904).

C. Doran. "First Submarine in Actual Warfare." *Confederate Veteran* (November 1908).

Ruth H. Duncan. *The Captain and Submarine CSS H. L. Hunley*. Memphis: S. C. Toof & Co., 1965.

Joseph T. Durkin. *Stephen R. Mallory: Confederate Navy Chief*. Chapel Hill: University of North Carolina Press, 1954.

Patricia L. Faust (ed.). *Historical Times Illustrated Encyclopedia of the Civil War*. New York: Harper & Row, 1986.

William M. Fowler, Jr. *Under Two Flags: The American Navy in the Civil War*. New York: Norton, 1990.

A. P. Ford. "The First Submarine Boat." *Confederate Veteran* (November 1908).

W. R. Fort. "First Submarine in the Confederate Navy." *Confederate Veteran* (October 1918).

Gary Gentile. *Ironclad Legacy*. Philadelphia: Gentile Productions, 1993.

George Hagerman. "Confederate Submarines." *U. S. Naval Institute Proceedings* (September 1977).

Brayton Harris (edited by Walter J. Boyne). *The Navy Times Book of Submarines: A Political, Social, and Military History*. New York: Berkley, 1997.

J. I. Hartwell. "An Alabama Hero." *Montgomery Advisor* (March 11, 1900).

E. S. Hearin. "*Hunley* Focal Point of Civil War Gathering." *Mobile Register* (February 2, 1989).

Chester G. Hearn. *Admiral David Glasgow Farragut: The Civil War Years*. Annapolis: Naval Institute Press, 1997.

H. N. Hill. "Texan Gave World First Successful

Submarine Torpedo." *San Antonio Express* (July 30, 1916).

Edwin P. Hoyt. *From the Turtle to the Nautilus: The Story of Submarines*. Boston: Little, Brown, 1963.

"Hunley Surfacing Worries Experts." *Charleston Post & Carrier* (May 21, 1995).

Alvah F. Hunter. (Edited by Craig L. Symonds.) *A Year on a Monitor and the Destruction of Fort Sumter*. Columbia: University of South Carolina Press, 1987.

Wallace Hutcheon. *Robert Fulton, Naval Warfare Genius*. Annapolis: Naval Institute Press, 1981.

H. Johnson. "Jeremiah Donivan, Survivor of *Hunley*, Died in His Bed." *Mobile Register* (November 19, 1948).

James E. Kloeppel. *Danger Beneath the Waves*. College Park, Ga.: Adele Enterprises, 1987.

Raimondo Luraghi. *A History of the Confederate Navy*. Annapolis: Naval Institute Press, 1996.

F. W. Lipscomb. *Historic Submarines*. New York: Praeger, 1969.

R. H. Little. "The First Submarine to Sink a Hostile Warship." *Chicago Tribune* (November 29, 1936).

Herbert R. Lottman. *Jules Verne: An Exploratory Biography*. New York: St. Martin's Press, 1996.

Horace S. Mazet. "Tragedy and the Confederate Submarines." *U. S. Naval Institute Proceedings* (May 1942).

Richard L. Maury. "The First Submarine Torpedoes." *Southern Historical Society Papers*. Vol. XXXI (1903).

Richard Knowles Morris. *John P. Holland: 1841-1914; Inventor of the Modern Submarine*. Annapolis: U. S. Naval Institute, 1966.

Ivan Musicant. *Divided Waters: The Naval History of the Civil War*. New York: Harper Collins, 1995.

"Navy Still Plans Hunt for *Hunley*." *Charleston News & Courier* (August 28, 1957).

John Niven. *Gideon Welles: Lincoln's Secretary of the Navy*. Baton Rouge: Louisiana State University Press, 1994.

Daniel O'Flaherty. "The Blockade that Failed." *American Heritage* (August 1955).

Charles H. Olmstead. "Charleston Harbor: Colonel Charles H. Olmstead's Reminiscences of Service in 1863." *Southern Historical Society Papers*. Vol. XI (Feb.–March 1883).

Gerard Patterson. "Gustave." *Civil War Times Illustrated* (July/August 1992).

Milton F. Perry. *Infernal Machines: The Story of Confederate Submarine and Mine Warfare*. Baton Rouge: Louisiana State University Press, 1965.

J. M. Powles. "*Hunley* Sinks the *Housatonic*!" *Navy Magazine* (January 1965).

Mark K. Ragan. *The Hunley: Submarines, Sacrifice, & Success in the Civil War*. Charleston, S. C.: Narwhal Press, 1995.

———. "Union and Confederate Submarine Warfare." *North & South* (March 1999).

William M. Robinson. *The Confederate Privateers*. Columbia: University of South Carolina Press, 1994.

Alex Roland. *Underwater Warfare in the Age of Sail*. Bloomington: Indiana University Press, 1978.

Robert N. Rosen. *Confederate Charleston: An Illustrated History of the City and the People During the Civil War*. Columbia: University of South Carolina Press, 1994.

"Salvage of Submarine *Hunley* Has Chance for Success." *Charleston News & Courier* (August 28, 1957).

Louis S. Schafer. *Confederate Underwater Warfare: An Illustrated History*. Jefferson, N. C.: McFarland & Co., 1996.

J. Thomas Scharf. *History of the Confederate States Navy*. Baltimore: Fairfax Press, 1887.

Richard F. Snow. "The 'Holland' Resurfaces." *American Heritage* (April 1984).

E. Lee Spence. *Treasures of the Confederate Coast: The Real "Rhett Butler" & Other Revelations*. Charleston, S. C.: Narwhal Press, 1995.

William N. Still Jr., John M. Taylor, and Norman C. Delaney. *Raiders and Blockaders: The American Civil War Afloat*. Dulles, Va.: Brassey's, 1998.

Ray Taylor. "The History of the Confederate Submarine Hunley and its Rediscovery." *Military Illustrated* (April 1995)

Sidney H. Schell. "Submarine Weapons Tested at Mobile During the Civil War." *Alabama Review* (July 1992).

Philip Van Doren Stern. *The Confederate Navy: A Pictorial History*. Garden City, N. Y.: Doubleday, 1962.

William N. Still, Jr. (ed.). *The Confederate Navy: The Ships, Men and Organization, 1861–1865*. Annapolis: Naval Institute Press, 1998.

James B. Sweeney. *A Pictorial History of Oceanographic Submersibles*. New York: Crown, 1970.

D. W. Thomson. "Three Confederate Submarines." *U. S. Naval Institute Proceedings* (January 1941).

"Treasury of Early Submarines (1775–1903)." *U. S. Naval Institute Proceedings* (May 1967).

Jules Verne (translated by Anthony Bonner). *Twenty Thousand Leagues Under the Sea*. New York: Bantam Books, 1962.

Voices of the Civil War: Charleston. Alexandria, Va.: Time-Life Books, 1997.

John C. Wideman. *Civil War Chronicles: Naval Warfare*. New York: Metro Books, 1997.

T. Harry Williams. *P. G. T. Beauregard: Napoleon in Gray*. Baton Rouge: Louisiana State University Press, 1955.

Stephen R. Wise. *Gate of Hell: Campaign for Charleston Harbor, 1863*. Columbia: University of South Carolina Press, 1994.

———. *Lifeline of the Confederacy: Blockade Running During the Civil War*. Columbia: University of South Carolina Press, 1991.

Recent Additions to Literature on the *H. L. Hunley*

R. Thomas Campbell. *The Hunley Story: Journey of a Confederate Submarine*. Shippensburg, Pa.: White Mane, 2002.

Brian Hicks and Schuyler Kropf. *Raising the Hunley: The Remarkable History and Recovery of the Lost Confederate Submarine*. New York: Ballantine, 2002.

Glenn Oeland. "The *H. L. Hunley*: Secret Weapon of the Confederacy." *National Geographic* (July 2002).

Rich Wills. "The *H. L. Hunley* in Historical Context." Naval Historical Center, *www.history.navy.mil*.

Photo Credits

OTHER
COOPER SQUARE PRESS
TITLES OF INTEREST

THE DAY LINCOLN WAS SHOT
An Illustrated Chronicle
Richard Bak
240 pp., b/w photos &
illustrations
0-87833-195-6
$18.95
0-87833-200-6
$29.95 cloth

ROUGH RIDERS
Theodore Roosevelt
With additional text
by Richard Bak
256 pp., b/w photos
throughout
0-87833-194-8
$18.95
0-87833-982-5
$29.95 cloth

LINDBERGH
Tragedy and Triumph
Richard Bak
256 pp., color & b/w photos
throughout
0-87833-246-4
$32.95 cloth

ROBERT E. LEE
A Life Portrait
David J. Eicher
240 pp., 380 b/w photos
0-87833-147-6
$19.95
0-87833-950-7
$29.95 cloth

THE SELECTED LETTERS OF
THEODORE ROOSEVELT
Edited by H. W. Brands
464 pp., 20 b/w photos and
illustrations
0-8154-1126-X
$32.00 cloth

THE BULLY PULPIT
A Teddy Roosevelt
Book of Quotations
H. Paul Jeffers
184 pp., 17 b/w illustrations
0-87833-149-2
$10.95
0-87833-999-X
$15.95 cloth

THE REBELS IN BLUE
The Story of Keith and
Malinda Blalock
Peter F. Stevens
256 pp., 18 b/w illustrations
0-87833-166-2
$24.95 cloth

THE ALAMO
An Illustrated History
Edwin P. Hoyt
208 pp., color & b/w photos
throughout
0-87833-204-9
$28.95 cloth

THE ALAMO
A Cultural History
Frank Thompson
272 pp., b/w photos
throughout
0-87833-254-5
$27.95

THAT'S NOT IN MY AMERICAN
HISTORY BOOK
A Compilation of Little-Known
Events and Forgotten Heroes
Thomas Ayres
256 pp., b/w photos &
illustrations
0-87833-185-9
$19.95 cloth

THE REVOLUTIONARY WAR QUIZ
AND FACT BOOK
Jonathan Hall
272 pp., b/w illustrations
throughout
0-87833-226-X
$14.95

THEY RODE FOR THE LONE STAR
The Saga of the Texas Rangers
Thomas W. Knowles
208 pp., 150 color & b/w
photos
0-87833-205-7
$29.95 cloth

STONEWALL JACKSON
A Life Portrait
K. M. Kostyal
224 pp., b/w photos
throughout
0-87833-220-0
$29.95 cloth

BEHIND ENEMY LINES
Civil War Spies, Raiders, and
Guerillas
Wilmer L. Jones, Ph.D
344 pp., b/w photos
throughout
0-87833-191-3
$26.95 cloth

DARK AND BLOODY GROUND
The Battle of Mansfield and the
Forgotten Civil War of Louisiana
Thomas Ayres
288 pp., b/w photo insert
0-87833-180-8
$24.95 cloth

ABRAHAM LINCOLN
Twentieth-Century
Popular Portrayals
Frank Thompson
304 pp., 100 b/w photos
0-87833-241-3
$26.95

AFTER THE THUNDER
Wilmer Jones, Ph.D.
368 pp., b/w photos
throughout
0-87833-176-X
$26.95 cloth

CONFEDERATE GENERALS
Life Portraits
George Cantor
208 pp., b/w photos
throughout
0-87833-179-4
$29.95 cloth